Effective E-Mail Marketing

Effective E-Mail Marketing

The Complete Guide to Creating Successful Campaigns

HERSCHELL GORDON LEWIS

AMACOM

American Management Association
New York • Atlanta • Brussels • Buenos Aires • Chicago • London • Mexico City
San Francisco • Shanghai • Tokyo • Toronto • Washington, D. C.

Special discounts on bulk quantities of AMACOM books are available to corporations, profes-
sional associations, and other organizations. For details, contact Special Sales Department,
AMACOM, a division of American Management Association,
1601 Broadway, New York, NY 10019.
Tel.: 212-903-8316. Fax: 212-903-8083.
Web site: www.amacombooks.org

This publication is designed to provide accurate and authoritative information in regard to the
subject matter covered. It is sold with the understanding that the publisher is not engaged in
rendering legal, accounting, or other professional service. If legal advice or other expert assis-
tance is required, the services of a competent professional person should be sought.

Library of Congress Cataloging-in-Publication Data
    Effective e-mail marketing: the complete guide to creating successful campaigns /
Herschell Gordon Lewis
        p. cm.
    Includes index.
ISBN 0-8144-7147-1
    1. Internet marketing. 2. Electronic mail systems. I. Title: E-mail marketing. II. Title:
E-mail marketing. III. Title.
    HF5415.1265 .L482 2002
    658.8′4—dc21   2002001933

Printing number

10 9 8 7 6 5 4 3

Contents

Preface

E-mail is the first force-communication phenomenon of the twenty-first century.

In a single package, we have total "one-to-one"—that is, total command of the recipient's attention. We also have complete capability of message testing and an unprecedented ease of transmission. (In fact, e-mail is an easier form of communication than speech, because the e-mail sender can catch and repair errors that readily slip out between the lips.)

But e-mail has a problem.

It is the problem that besets any apparently simple success story: Everybody—*everybody*—is an expert. And do you know what happens when everybody is an expert? Mistakes compound themselves because we so-called experts don't recognize mistakes *as mistakes*.

What types of mistakes that will reduce response and revenue might the commercial e-mail sender commit? Even a preliminary list is formidable:

- Overmailing (see Chapter 4)

- Undermailing (see Chapter 14)

- Using dull descriptions (see Chapter 11)

- Sending the identical message repeatedly (see Chapter 13)

- Not knowing the demographic of your targets (see Chapter 6)

- Not making *rapport* the key of every message (see Chapter 5)

- Assuming all your targets share the same demographic/psychographic profile (see Chapter 1)

- Eliminating target groups merely because you don't think they might respond (see Chapter 6)

- Refusing to test (see Chapter 1)

- Assuming that what works for direct mail automatically works for e-mail (see Chapter 2)

And that is just a starter list. But yes, mistakes are there to be made. And mistakes in e-mail invariably reduce response and revenue.

Are you reading this in the year 2004? Three years earlier Jupiter Research predicted that by this year, e-mail would command 15 percent of all advertising dollars. Were they overenthusiastic or too conservative?

Are you reading this in the year 2005? Then you can determine whether a prediction made four years earlier by IDC of Framingham, Massachusetts, is valid: that by 2005 there will be 35 billion commercial e-mail messages *per day*. That's nothing: The same source says total e-mails—personal as well as business—will be 9.2 *trillion*. And remember, personal e-mails fight for attention against commercial e-mails. Talk about competition! You had better be an expert.

Are you reading this in the year 2006? Then you may dismiss as an anecdote a "study" by Forrester Research that predicted by 2006, 40 percent of people who have at least four years of Internet-surfing experience would generally ignore e-mail marketing. Do you agree with that? I don't. This so-called study not only deals in opinions rather than results but also parallels someone saying he or she is bored with television, doesn't read a newspaper, or has no interest in sex.

If you don't care about reduced response and revenue, this book isn't for you. If you care about reduced response and revenue, I promise you'll find a nugget here and there that will more than justify the leap of faith you took when picking up this book in the first place.

And oh, before I forget: If you're looking for a book loaded with technical terms, impenetrable acronyms, and arcane terminology, this isn't it. This is a book about e-mail *marketing*—which makes it possible for those term-throwers to exist at all.

—Herschell Gordon Lewis
Fort Lauderdale, Florida

Acknowledgments

I am deeply indebted to Jock Bickert of The Looking Glass. This astute marketer, who developed the "Cohorts" segmentation that has repeatedly produced quantum leaps in response, not only made invaluable suggestions but also allowed me to test multiple e-mail concepts and then shared the results and analyses with me.

For the same reason, I offer my gratitude to Carol Bond of Carol Bond Health Foods, and Joel Irwin and Mark Irace of Proflowers.com. These intelligent marketers have shown a willingness to test e-mail copy and techniques, and I have profited mightily from being involved in the creation of their e-mailings.

Robert Dunhill of Dunhill International Lists and Jay Schwedelson of Worldata, both knowledgeable experts, graciously shared some of their own e-mail experiences with me.

Steve Hardigree, the marketing expert who heads Opt In Inc., is responsible for opening my eyes to many of the innovations for which he can claim origination.

My aquisitions editor at AMACOM Books, Ellen Kadin, is the principal reason this book appears at all. She has shown the kind of wisdom and patience an author—especially an author of a trade book—seldom has the pleasure of experiencing. I also salute her endurance.

To those venues that have allowed me to speak and conduct e-mail workshops—especially Direct Marketing Days, New York

(Tom Turner), the Detroit Direct Marketing Association (David Marold), and Direct Media's Conference (Neil Lichtman)—I am grateful on two levels: first, for the opportunity to compare ideas and results; and second, for the comments and critiques that always help to refine my opinions and conclusions.

To those who know how I live and work, one acknowledgment is both obvious and crucial: My wife, Margo, has been my partner in this project, as she has been in many prior books. Whether it is forwarding an unusually effective or unusually foul e-mail . . . or pointing out an unwarranted prejudice in the text . . . or simply keeping me sane, I have no words that can adequately express my gratitude to her for putting up with me.

Bless you and thank you, one and all.

HGL

(A clarifying note about examples reprinted in the text: Except for e-mails sent to my household, I've scrambled the recipients' online addresses for reasons of privacy. Each example is genuine, as sent.)

Effective E-Mail Marketing

Effective E-Mail— The Communications Revolution

Let's start with a quick question: "How many different media do you need to personalize, adapt to individual groups, test price, determine whether straight text generates more response than a produced message, test message length, be able to read results within one or two days, test incentives, differentiate messages to business from messages to consumers, and provide hundreds of demographic splits?"

You know the answer: "One."

E-mail, to astute marketers, ranks right up there with the Gutenberg Bible and television as a quantum leap forward in the art—or, more in sync with the twenty-first century, the *science*—of communication. Make that *force*-communication, because we, in this environment, aren't concerned with noncommercial messages. (But we certainly are concerned with commercial messages we don't want to look unprofessional.)

E-mail represents the culmination of a communications revolution that began with the telephone—supplementing, augmenting, and eventually replacing natural one-to-one relationships with bulk, manufactured, artificial one-to-one pseudorelationships. Refinements, following those of telephone marketing, focus on preventing the potential customer, client, or donor from recognizing the prefix "pseudo-."

E-Mail Offers Advantages to Marketers

Even during the early experimental period, successful and astute e-mail marketers realized that no previous medium offered the advantages e-mail brings to the marketing arena. While other dot-com start-ups flared with egotistical self-promotion before flaming out, e-marketers charted a steady course, spending so little on each contact that failure was harder to achieve than success.

But I said, *successful* and *astute* e-mailers. Those qualifiers thin the ranks considerably, because successful and astute e-mailers quickly see the value of testing. They tabulate test results exactly the way expensive (but in this case unnecessary) researchers would tabulate them. Then, unlike career researchers, they quickly implement the results of their research, constantly alert to changing market conditions that might dictate a change in course.

All this may strike you as primitive. I hope it does because that means you accept testing and *skeptical* acceptance of test results as an absolute necessity for successful e-marketing.

Testing Is Crucial

Let's accept that a generic characteristic of the World Wide Web—not only e-mail but the Web as a marketing medium—can be explained in one sentence: The Web is price-driven.

Oh, certainly exceptions exist. But those exceptions are based on the most elusive of all Web relationships: *loyalty*. To crack the marketplace—as one chooses among the motivators that might get a positive mouse-click—the combination of exclusivity (a natural element in what appears to be a personalized communication) and discounted price (a necessary element in the most competitive marketplace ever developed) has yet to be beaten, and may never be.

Price testing is the most common test. A suggestion, when you are testing price, don't test $24.95 against $29.95. Cross over to the next ten. So, it would be $29.95 against $39.95. For larger numbers, bring the discount below the intervening hundred. As in, "Regularly $249. Yours this week only for $189." Which brings us to the second testing element: expiration date.

TIP

Note the use of the phrase "this week only" because I may point it out several times in this book. An expiration date always helps response. And the more specific the expiration date, the better the response. So, "Reply by midnight, Friday, May 25" has greater power than "Reply by Friday, May 25," which in turn has greater power than "Reply by May 25."

Although the Web is price-driven, don't limit your incentive programs to whatever you may have in your warehouse. Test incentives against one another. Sweepstakes and newsletters are used nearly as often as straight discounts. (We'll discuss newsletters frequently in this text because the term *newsletter* is often a mask or wrapping for commercial messages.) Merchandise ranging from pens and letter openers to baseballs and mouse pads are popu-

TIP

When recruiting customers, clients, or donors, keep the message short. Message length can increase in ratio to the number of times the prospect has contacted you.

lar incentives. Free shipping is often the runaway winner in an incentives test. And that is what you should do: Test.

A fourth element worthy of testing is message length. Chapter 2 describes some of the basic rules for e-mail messages. In this chapter, we're concerned about the benefits of short messages versus long messages.

And of course technology has to play a part. Should you take the cheap and easy course by using straight text? Or should you use the more expensive, time-consuming, and lavish HTML or the visual and auditory splendor of rich mail? The answer is obvious: Test.

Just be sure, when you test, that the test groups are parallel when you test. Don't test one message to your list of prior buyers against a message to a group of semi-interested names who don't know you but unwittingly subscribed to a newsletter on which your message coattail-rides.

CPM Is Replaced by CPA

For generations, marketers have paid homage to three initials: CPM. As almost everyone associated with advertising knows, the initials stand for "cost per thousand." (M is the Roman numeral for 1,000.)

Publications traditionally based their rate cards on CPM. Broadcast stations, while not always using the initials, employed the same procedure, by using rating points that equate to the number of viewers or listeners.

In my opinion, CPM is not only obsolete today, it was obsolete from the beginning. Smart marketers don't want to reach the largest number of people. They want to reach the largest number of people who can and might respond.

This led to the evolution of a new set of initials: CPA. Originally, CPA was an acronym for "cost per acquisition," but recently it has changed to the more dynamic and flexible "cost per action." The benefit to marketers is obvious: They pay only for response, not for raw exposure.

Steve Hardigree, CEO of Opt In Inc., has been a CPA pioneer. He writes:

E-mail marketing as an advertising medium will become one of the dominant resources for the "click and mortar" companies of the new millennium. And due to its relatively low cost, personalization, and tracking capabilities, it will be the choice of direct marketers across all vertical markets.

The cost of e-mail marketing will shift from a CPM model to a CPA or CPA/CPM hybrid, forcing e-mail marketing firms to become participants in the creation and design of e-mail campaigns in order to benefit in a true "pay for performance" relationship. As a result, e-mail marketing firms will have to put more sophisticated technology in place to ensure that traffic generated via their promotions is accounted for (i.e. pixel tracking, 800 number, open rates, click rates, and similar criteria).

Is the CPA model the e-mail giant of the future? Many marketers hope so because when the medium becomes a salesperson, the monetary compensation is then structured in the way most major retailers structure their compensation—as a commission-based arrangement.

The Medium Is New, The Intention Isn't

Have you used e-mail for any of these:

- The announcement of special offers, available only by the e-mail connection?

- Referrals to previous purchases or activities?

- Regular hotline clearance sales?

- Frequent-buyer programs?

- Easy-to-win contests with discount coupons as prizes?

- Unexpected rewards?

If you haven't, you may have missed an extra opportunity to solidify a relationship that otherwise might be so fragile it can break.

Marketers who separate e-mail from the rest of the marketing mix are either unaware of a truism or are ignoring it: The customers and contacts haven't changed. They are the same people you would want to reach if e-mail didn't exist. Whether by e-mail, direct mail, television, or on the inside of matchbook covers, success comes from reaching and influencing—at the lowest possible cost—the largest number of people who can and will respond to your offer.

What e-mail has given the world of force-communication is a quantum leap in timing, an astounding reduction in cost, and an automatic one-to-one relationship. Oh, yes, these are gigantic improvements, but they don't change the *intention*.

Which means what?

It means that in e-mail, as in television and printing, technology should be subordinate to principles of psychology. The most expensive method may not be the most effective.

TIP

In e-mails to business, a rich media or "produced" message may be less effective than straight text. Why? Because straight text is less likely to present the immediate advertising impression, "I want to sell you something."

A Gartner Inc. study indicated that at least 34 percent of business e-mails do not contain content employees need to perform their jobs. The number becomes significant when integrated with another statistic: 25 percent of the employees surveyed for this study spend more than an hour each business day going through, or "managing," e-mails. The average time spent on e-mails was forty-nine minutes.

A Few Case Histories

Rockport Company LLC, a division of Reebok, decided to build an e-mail list of opt-ins.

The company sent a sweepstakes offer—a safari in Kenya—to 200,000 names, some of which were already registered, but many of which were bought from a list company. Rockport reported a 6 percent click-through—12,000—which eventually boiled down to between 3,000 and 4,000 registrants.

Subsequently, Rockport sent e-mails to 250,000 names, again for a sweepstakes—this time for a vacation at an Arizona spa. Included were 20,000 so-called "house names"—names from existing Rockport lists. The company anticipated 8,000 to 10,000 registrants, announcing it would continue to mix bought names and house names for ongoing e-mails.

Borders initiated a series of promotional e-mails called Borders Store Exclusives, sent either monthly or bimonthly to brick-and-mortar customers whose e-mail addresses are on file. (The collection of the names, said to be in excess of one million, was done at the stores, where customers were asked to sign up for newsletters and exclusives.) The typical promotion is a 20 percent discount coupon valid at any of the more than three hundred Borders stores.

The chain reported a double-digit response, plus a click-through rate of almost 30 percent on a forward-to-a-friend button, which enables customers to send the same coupon to another person. These results show an unusually successful venture into the online referral technique of viral mail (see Chapter 16).

Borders also says it segments its mailings by targeted newsletters, such as *Borders Business Class* and *Borders Lit,* based on its customer database.

Freelotto.com has held a series of lotteries that promise major prizes, including the possibility of up to $11 million each day. When visitors register, they are asked to provide information that goes well beyond their online names.

E-mailed advertising to registrants underwrites the monetary prizes, and Freelotto has been able to offer advertisers the possibility of sophisticated targeting based on demographics stemming from the registration information.

TIP

If you have a sweepstakes or prize offer, plug it on your home page. Don't assume that e-mail announcements alone will seize the attention of every name on the list. Get interaction any way you can, because interaction is the key to gaining the customer's often fragile attention to your next e-mail.

The Radical Mail Lesson

A company that flared like a rocket . . . and quickly flared out like a spent rocket . . . was Radical Mail, whose streaming video and audio were state of the art. Once regarded as the king of rich media, Radical Mail went out of business in mid-2001.

What happened? Chapter 16 explores the circumstances. I'll mention at this point, however, that the outcome of the story serves as a warning to all e-communicators: E-mail has to motivate. If it entertains, that's frosting on the cake. But it has to motivate, regardless of whether or not it's entertaining. Now, how about the reverse? Does it have to entertain, whether it motivates or not? The Radical Mail story, as told later in this book, will answer that question.

Adapting Your Message to This Medium

Remember Where You Are

Part of e-mail's power is inherent in the medium itself. People turn on their computers and deliberately check who has contacted them since the last time they logged on . . . which could have been only half an hour before.

Newspaper and magazine subscribers usually don't buy these publications because they want to see advertising. Television viewers dislike commercials so intently that gadgets designed for cutting out the commercials enjoy a brisk sale. Direct mail, the incestuous first cousin of e-mail, comes unannounced as does commercial e-mail, but it lacks the cachet of the glamorous new medium.

Just by being there with their fingers on a mouse, your e-mail targets signal that they expect you. Do they welcome you? The subject line and first sentence answer that question quickly.

You can see the creative significance of the differential. If you just retype your direct mail letter, you've ignored where you are. Direct mail may be delivered Monday or a week from Thursday. Except for overnight courier, the printed message can't begin to match the immediacy of the e-mail message. (Nor can it begin to match its low cost.) The statement, "You have only three days left," makes sense in e-mail, but not in snail mail.

Although the statement, "You have only three days left," also retains timeliness in newspapers and broadcast media, there are two deficiencies. First, the means of immediate response isn't at hand; and second, the one-to-one aspect isn't there.

TIP

The bulk of consumer response to advertising usually arrives within forty-eight hours. That's faster than business response, because business recipients typically aren't as likely to dedicate time for immediate response, especially on Mondays and Fridays. (See Chapter 15.)

Impatience Demands Specifics

Nothing is leisurely about the Web. The mouse is merciless, and boredom is always a threat.

An ancient principle of force-communication is: Get to the point. This principle must prevail if you want your message to be read . . . and to generate a response.

Accepting that principle means accepting the corollary that dominates much of this book's philosophy: Specifics outpull generalizations.

Figure 2-1 is an offer for golf balls. It's perfectly adjusted to the mentality of Web visitors because it's absolutely specific, with no embellishments and no wasted adjectives. This straightforward message is in tune with the short attention span, impatience, and demand for specificity that typifies someone looking at the day's e-mail. Would illustrations and slicker production increase the effectiveness of this e-mail? In my opinion, illustrations and production would damage it by softening the "right now" aspect.

Figure 2-1. Do you need any golf balls?

Subj:	**Do You Need Any Golf Balls ??**
Date:	5:48:37 PM Pacific Standard Time
From:	ballman@sendmegolfballs.com
Reply-to:	ballman@sendmegolfballs.com
To:	someone3@aol.com

We Are Currently Offering Great Prices On All Our Titleist Products

Call Us For Additional Information.

		Item #
Titleist Professional	$22.95 doz	RHS11T
Titleist Prestige	$23.95 doz	RHS17T
Titleist Tour Distance	$19.95 doz	RHS13T
Titleist HP Tours	$14.95 doz	RHS12T
Titleist HP Distance	$15.95 doz	RD31T
Tilteist HP Eclipse	$16.95 doz	RM32T
Titleist HVC	$12.95 doz	RD32T
Titleist DT	$11.95 doz	RM20T
Titleist Professional Blems	$69.95 10-doz	SP06TP
Titleist Mixed Blems	$39.95 10-doz	SP07TM

These are our superb premium quality golf balls, the finest quality we have available. These are NOT X-OUTS. Call us for more details.

Other great values include:

Strata	$16.95 doz	RHS16T
MaxFli Revolution	$19.95 doz	RHS15
Nike	$19.95 doz	RMS21N
Taylor Made InnerGels	$23.95 doz	RD46TA
Precept MC	$14.95 doz	RHS20P
Precept EV Spin or Distance	$14.95 doz	RMS24
Staff Titanium Distance or Spin	$13.95 doz	RD38W

(continues)

Figure 2-1. (*continued*)

Pinnacle Xtreme	$ 9.95 doz	RD40P
Top Flite Magna	$ 9.95 doz	RD34TF
Slazenger Raw or Spin	$16.95 doz	RD36S
Top Flite XL 2000-all models	$ 9.95 doz	RD35TF
Ultras	$ 9.95 doz	RD37U
MaxFli MD	$ 8.95 doz	RMS26M
Pinnacle Gold	$ 6.95 doz	RD41PN
Top Flite XL	$ 6.95 doz	RD35TF
Prostaff	$59.95 10-doz	SP08PS

Call us if you don't see your favorite ball.

We have nearly every kind of ball imaginable, usually at less than half of manufacturer's suggested list. We also carry a fabulous selection of women's golf balls, senior's balls and optical yellow balls.

3 doz min order
Add $1.50 per doz shipping and handling.
No sales tax unless you live in Texas (Tex residents add 8.25%).
Most orders UPS delivered within 5 days.
All Credit Cards Accepted

Call 888-205-4059 to order by credit card, 281-561-5033 for check-fax orders. Or call 281-560-0132 from outside the US.

Call us for a complete catalog or for additional information.

Call 8am to 10pm Central Time -Including Weekends- for information or to place an order.

Best Wishes For Great Golf
Dana Jones
Remember - The Ballman Saves You Money
888-205-4059
281-560-0132

Asking for Information? Be Careful

Figure 2-2 exemplifies a problem many e-mails self-generate. These e-mails shroud specificity combining a muzzy offer with a request for a considerable amount of personal information. An example would help this generalized offer. Anyone in a heavy-debt position has seen many such propositions. The ones that bring response are those that include examples with which the individual can identify.

Figure 2-2. Consolidate your debt.

Subj:	**CONSOLIDATE YOUR DEBT (ITS My Final Answer) [9ma4o]**
Date:	6:10:07 PM Pacific Daylight Time
From:	rz6qp9q41@msn.com
Reply-to:	lonstepp38@publicist.com
To:	rmjnn6@msn.com

How would you like to take all of your debt, reduce or eliminate the interest, pay less per month, and pay them off sooner?

We have helped over 20,000 people do just that.

If you are interested, we invite you request our free information by provide the following information.

Full Name:
Address:
City:
State:
Zip Code:
Home Phone:
Work Phone:
Best Time to Call:
E-Mail Address:

(*continues*)

Figure 2-2. (*continued*)

Estimated Debt Size:

(All information is kept securely and never
provided to any third party sources)

This request is totally risk free.
No obligation or costs are incurred.

To unsubscribe please hit reply and send a message with
remove in the subject.

Desperate people might grab the lifeline this e-mail represents, but they are the poorest, most unqualified prospects. Those who want relief but aren't in desperate need of it would be uneasy about revealing the amount of their personal debt to an unknown source. In that respect, this type of offer differs from an identical offer printed in a more dispassionate and more impersonal medium, such as a newspaper. That's because the individual wouldn't feel singled out for analysis.

Instead of asking for both home and business telephone numbers and estimated debt size, what else might be done before making a commitment or specific promise? A statement of inclusion might have helped, such as, "If your current debt is between $2,000 and $20,000, by all means respond to this invitation."

Figure 2-3 is a parallel offer that more closely recognizes the personal nature of an e-mail message. Compare this message with Figure 2-2. Note the specificity and care used to project the benefit to the recipient, without creating a feeling of embarrassment. Assuming you're interested in a loan but aren't aggressively seeking one, which of the two e-mails makes you feel more comfortable?

Figure 2-3. Do you owe money?

Subj:	**Do you owe money? [g5d72]**
Date:	1:23:10 PM Eastern Daylight Time
From:	wwk104i@msn.com
Reply-to:	jenaepratcher4517@excite.com
To:	w2pejw@msn.com

Do you owe money? Is it getting troublesome keeping track
of all those bills and whom you owe how much and when? Would
it not be easier if you could just make 1 monthly payment
instead of several? We can help!

If your debts are $4,000 US or more and you are a United
States citizen, you can consolidate your debt into just one
easy payment! You do not have to own a home, nor do you need
to take out a loan. Credit checks are not required!

To receive more information regarding our services, please
fill out the form below and return it to us, or provide the
necessary information in your response. There are absolutely
no obligations. All the fields below are required for your
application to be processed.

****

Full Name :
Address :
City :
State :
Zip Code :
Home Phone :
Work Phone :
Best Time to Call :
E-Mail Address :
Estimated Debt Size :

(continues)

Figure 2-3. (*continued*)

```
**********

Please allow up to ten business days for application
processing.

Thank You

Note: If this e-mail arrived to you by error, or you wish
to never receive such advertisements from our company,
please reply to this e-mail with the word REMOVE in the
e-mail subject line. We apologize for any inconveniences
```

The Two Rules of Interactivity

A current buzzword is *interactivity*, and e-mail certainly qualifies as one of the two interactive media. (The other is telemarketing—misused even more than e-mail.)

Consider the two Rules of Interactivity when structuring e-mail commercial messages. The first rule:

1. Desire is linked to benefit. So emphasize benefit in the subject line.

The second rule:

2. Perception of benefit decreases in exact ratio to perception of necessary effort—work.

That's a nasty four-letter word in e-mail: *w-o-r-k*. We all have seen e-mails with wording such as, "If you work hard, you'll . . ." or "Rewards will come if you work to achieve them." The statements may be true, but they don't reflect a sense of sales expertise.

This is true for many areas beside e-mail. People bear pain better when they have been preconditioned to see a benefit after the pain.

Without the preconditioning, they're resentful, angry, or bewildered—none of which is a positive reaction.

Let's look at controlled circulation subscription renewals, as an example. Many business publications—especially those in computer-related fields—offer an online renewal option. As often as not, the renewal notification comes by e-mail, since these publications have collected e-mail addresses as a condition of the original subscription. Some of the questions, easily answered on paper, seem endless online. Check . . . click . . . check . . . click . . . come on, when does this end? Aw, I don't need that magazine anyway. And a renewal vanishes because the publication, dedicated to its own field of interest, forgets where it is.

Customizing the Message to the Medium

Should you put your company name in the subject line? Your brand name?

Most consultants and advertising agencies say yes.

But hold it!

Here is where I outrage another possibly innocent group. E-mail is generically different from other mass media. Consultants and agencies working for you may have an agenda that differs from yours. They may feel you really prefer massaging your ego to establishing and/or maintaining rapport with your customers.

(Would you put "A message from our chairman" on your Web site's home page? If you would, I hope you're my competitor.)

The decision about whether or not to put your company name in the subject line never should be absolute. It should be based on the logic that underlies every effective advertising message. Does your company or brand name hold great sig-

TIP

The key question in deciding whether or not to put your company name in the subject line is to ask: Where did you get this person's address?

nificance for your targets? Is that significance the most attention-grabbing facet of the communication you're sending? The question answers itself.

If you're an astute marketer, you know something about every name on your list. That person has told you—or, less dependably, told an outside source—about his or her interests, or age, or profession, or background, or travels, or lifestyle . . . or all of the above. Milk those interests.

Tailoring the message to the individual not only is easier in e-mail than in any other medium but also is vital for maximized success. And the definition of maximized success is unconditional: conversion of visitor to customer, customer to advocate.

More than any other medium, e-mail depends on instant positive attention. Think like the message recipient, not the message sender, and the key to your subject line will become apparent.

Holding Onto Business Prospects

Figure 2-4 is a typical business-to-business solicitation. Typically, the writer forgets where he or she is. The subject line is a question whose content is general rather than specific. The message is slow to make its point and is too long. What has happened here? The writer has forgotten that this is an e-mail.

Figure 2-4. Want to develop great managers?

Subj:	**Want to Develop GREAT Managers?**
Date:	7:55:11 AM Pacific Standard Time
From:	BillComm.632@info.dbasenews.com (MOHR Learning)
To:	hglewis1@aol.com

MOHR LEARNING
PART OF THE PROVANT SOLUTION

What do you worry about most?

Employee retention?   Customer loyalty?   Increasing sales?

It's no secret that these issues are connected. In fact, a recent Harvard research study proved that a 5% increase in employee loyalty creates a 1.3% increase in customer loyalty. This ultimately creates a .5 percent increase in profitability!

What's the key to making this happen? Great managers ... ones who can create powerful results while developing their people. These are managers who know how to:

* Listen to and communicate with employees
* Reinforce employees' performance
* Develop employees to their maximum potential
* Manage by asking and coaching, versus
  telling and directing

Now is the time to transformgood managers into GREAT managers.

Whether it's first-line supervisors or higher-level managers, MOHR Learning's Retail Management Series (RMSIII) can provide your managers with the skills they need to be successful.

No need to customize this program for your retail environment. RMSIII was developed for retail merchants by MOHR Learning's instructional designers who understand your needs because they, themselves, are experienced retailers. Delivered at your site or by certifying your trainers, the program can be taught all at once or in modules tailored to your specific needs, time frames, and populations.
                Contact us today:
mohrinfo@mohrlearning.com (201-670-1001)

                Visit our web site:
www.mohrlearning.com

(*continues*)

Figure 2-4. (*continued*)

This message is brought to you as a valued subscriber to
Bill Communications. Please note, Bill Communications is
not affiliated with this offer. To remove your name
from the list, click here:

http://unsub.ed4.net/unsub1/13/3/139/139/11392/gen/aGdsZXdpcz
FAYW9sLmNvbQ==/

[[11392]]

Online attention spans are short, and that truth, repeated so often (but never too often) in this text, eludes writers who think in terms of direct mail or space ads or even broadcast, where one can build up to the point of the message. E-mail to a business prospect does not differ from e-mail to a consumer prospect—get to the point fast . . . and be sure there *is* a point that can be immediately recognized as beneficial to the reader.

The example in Figure 2-4 runs on too long to hold the reader's interest. It parallels asking too much of the consumer at the shopping cart. Although questions are automatically reader involving, the subject line, "Want to develop GREAT managers?" is weak. Even "Do your managers worry you?" would be a better grabber.

Synergy Doesn't Mean Direct Pickups

The synergy between direct mail and e-mail not only exists, it sparkles with energy.

The differences are obvious. Because of its various components of writing, producing, printing, and mailing, direct mail can require a month or more of lead time and weeks for evaluating responses. E-mail can be written this morning and evaluated tomorrow.

Another obvious difference is cost. The dramatically lower cost of e-mail makes it an economical testing medium, which is why an increasing number of conventional mailers are reversing the usual procedure of using e-mail as a follow-up to direct mail. Instead, marketers are now using e-mail to pretest the appeal, the results of which are used for structuring the more expensive direct-mail package. This helps to bring response more in line, because direct mail, unhelped, usually won't deliver as high a percentage of results as e-mail.

The parallels between direct mail and e-mail are equally obvious. Each of these types of direct media depends on the exquisite LOCK mixture of *list, offer, creative*, and *know-how* for success. The first two elements are parallel. A marketer needs to be astute in choosing not only the lists but also the list provider. The offer has to match what the selected demographic/psychographic profile indicates as a need for improving the receptivity of buyers.

The creative approach may be parallel, but for maximum impact probably isn't. Direct mail not only offers the opportunity to move back and forth among these four elements, but it may actually encourage it. The linear nature of e-mail demands an arrowed buildup with multiple reminders.

E-mail know-how includes not only a working knowledge of technical and mechanical options and how to use them, but also the more significant knowledge of where we are—in a wild bazaar. Jupiter Communications reported that more than two thirds of e-mail marketing recipients respond best to promotions and value-related offers. In my opinion, that percentage is low . . . but if we accept the data, we have to conclude that safety lies in recognizable incentives for fast action, such as coupons and discounts with short expiration dates.

Using Reverses, Serifs, and Other Minutiae

Do you believe that reverse type is difficult to read and causes eye strain? Well, it does . . . sort of. But don't eschew reverses only because of this common perception. Instead, remember where you are—in e-mail. My Web site is loaded with reverses, but I don't use reverses in e-mails except where they're part of an unchangeable corporate image.

How About Sans-Serif Type?

Many search engines use Arial 10-point typeface as their default, which is a pleasant but nondescript sans-serif typeface. Some suppliers caution against using a specific typeface such as Goudy or Palatino, because the recipient's computer may change the font. So what? The majority of computers will deliver the message as it was sent.

How About Blue or Red Type?

For emphasis, why not use blue or red type? But if you use it for emphasis, remember one of the Great Laws of force-communication: When you emphasize everything, you emphasize nothing.

TIP

Sending an entire text message in an unusual color will seize attention. The trade-off is that the message is quickly recognizable as advertising. Whether this is a positive or negative effect depends entirely on your relationship with the recipient.

Revisiting an Ancient Rule

This rule of direct response is at least a century old: Concentrate the offer and sell just one thing, one item, one concept, one request for positive attention.

E-mail is this century's embodiment of that rule. Sell just one thing, one item, one concept, or one request for positive attention. Aside from the obvious benefit of completely focused attention, e-mail, optimally, is antidiversion. If you have two offers, what could be easier than sending two e-mails, so the impact of each is not diluted.

But, if the offer is one in which a discount applies for multiple choices, it still is considered a single offer, as is an offer for flowers that includes half a dozen bouquets from which to choose.

But the rule is absolute. From an attention-grabbing point of view, an offer of a dozen roses at a special price is more dynamic than an offer of a dozen roses or a dozen tulips or a dozen carnations at special prices.

Optimizing the Medium

The Drexel furniture company decided to send an electronic brochure, complete with video, to Web visitors who had signed the online guest book and agreed to receive future e-communications. Drexel created an e-brochure, a highly compressed rich media approach that recipients had to download. The e-brochure was personalized with each recipient's name and included a link to a printable coupon for 10 percent off any item in a Drexel Heritage store. It also included a thirty-second video of showrooms, with links to DrexelHeritage.com, and a store-locator option.

The company e-mailed 22,000 e-brochures, of which 2,000 went to people who opted in for Drexel Heritage e-mail by signing a guest book on the Web site during the previous eight months. A spokesperson said that 21 percent of this group opened the e-mail.

E-mailings to an additional 2,000 names collected in the four weeks prior to each subsequent drop date yielded a 26 to 27 percent response. These results obviously were considerably better than might be expected from a direct-mail effort, whose response typically would be below 3 percent.

Since Drexel's e-brochure wasn't streaming video, the recipients' Web browsers or connection speeds had no effect on its transmission quality. The company said 60 to 70 percent of recipients clicked through to locate their nearest dealer, and more than half passed the e-brochure on to others, making the viral mail aspect of this e-mailing, if factual, extraordinarily successful. Drexel said one recipient brought her brochure to a store in Atlanta early the next business day, and coupons were redeemed in other cities around the country. The recognition of recipient visits to stores prompted ongoing updates of the company's Web site.

Using Transactive E-Mail

Transactive e-mail, which is one of numerous Internet-generated terms, means that customers record their credit card information only once, making it possible to complete a fairly sophisticated transaction without linking to a Web site. The e-mail message becomes self-supporting.

User reaction is mixed, as it is for many facets of e-mail. The two major criticisms are:

1. The interactive environment invites people to search for the best value, which would discourage a one-step close.

2. Transactive e-mail becomes a difficult procedure for multi-product marketers such as cataloguers who prefer to lure prospects to their Web site for exposure to other items.

E-Mailing to the Mature Market

Should you tailor your message differently for seniors?

After all, we're talking not only about 40 percent of the population but also about the fastest-growing segment of Internet visitors. For example, between 1997 and 2001, the over-50 online presence grew by 65 percent. And seniors spend more time online than younger surfers, averaging more than thirty-eight hours each month.

But most important to e-mail marketers is the spending power of this group. They have money—55 percent of discretionary spending in the United States.

Just one problem: They aren't homogenized. There are seniors . . . and there are *seniors*.

How Far Over Age 50?

From a generational point of view, marketers can identify three distinct senior groups.

The first is the Baby Boomers. They are in their 50s to early 60s. Many of them—no, make that *most* of them—are still working. From a marketing viewpoint, they're the primary targets because, except for discounted meals at Denny's, they don't associate with their elders.

The second group is the mid-60s to mid-70s batch. They offer two distinctions: First, they probably have more leisure time, much of which can be spent online. Second, once they are past age 65, they can have pensions or Social Security or both—which, depending on what and how you market, can be a blessing or a curse.

The third group is the oldsters, those over age 75. Don't dismiss them out of hand as geezers, especially if what you sell relates to health and longevity. Too, this group is the one most likely to appreciate the benefit of being able to shop without leaving home.

TIP

Mirror print advertising from a production point of view when e-mailing to seniors. That means, above all, easily readable fonts. (Not a bad idea for e-mailing to everybody, provided it still looks like e-mail.) But don't make the mistake of letting your image be one of catering exclusively to elderly people. They will resent the suggestion as much as younger prospects might, albeit on a different level.

What Do the Three Senior Groups Have in Common?

The principal factor uniting all three senior groups is seasoning. They have had years of exposure to information, years of evaluating advertising claims, years in which they—or someone they knew— were cheated by misleading advertising.

The following three elements seem to be essential for success when e-mail is aimed at the senior market:

1. Whatever is being offered solves a problem.

2. A tie to stability helps overcome any implicit skepticism.

3. Suggesting a discount caters to senior expectations.

(TIP)

Excessive tailoring and excessive targeting can suppress response, not only from the fringes but also from the group at whom the message is targeted, because they may feel the communication is an invasion of privacy.

How Do the Three Senior Groups Differ?

Lines blur as marketing shifts from the youngest to the oldest seniors. But logical conclusions suggest these differentials:

The youngest group not only doesn't resist offers of life insurance, it looks for such offers, usually on a comparative-price basis. The oldest group seldom is worth circularizing for life insurance, not only because rates are prohibitively high for many seniors but also because many in this group either have paid-up insurance or see no further value in it.

The youngest group may be the best of all demographic segments for weight loss programs, with a response ratio even higher than for people in their 30s and 40s.

Collectibles and nostalgia-related items, such as publications with a historical connotation, seem to have the biggest appeal to the middle group. These are folks who look back as much as they look forward. They often want evidence of times past.

One would think the promotion of health supplements, health-related newsletters, and products claiming to increase longevity and to fight physical degeneration increase in effectiveness as age increases. That isn't universally true. Some marketers of supplements aimed at prostate problems or osteoporosis or gallstones report the highest degree of success among those just entering the senior classification.

The apparent benefit of marketing at a distance becomes more significant for the oldest group. Exploiting this benefit isn't as powerful as the two common denominators, but it always is worth marketing attention.

And what are the common denominators? One is price, or an apparent bargain. Many businesses offer discounts to senior citizens, not only because discounts are a tested and accepted business practice but also because seniors begin to expect such treatment. In e-mail, where the marketer has mere seconds to make a point, quick attention to price is sound marketing.

The other common denominator is the desire to be—or at least to be thought of as—ten years younger.

Catering to these two elements has another advantage: The appeal goes well beyond the over-50s.

Achieving Dynamic Personalization

Several of the chapters of this book include discussions of personalization— a key to improving response rates.

Experience seems to have proved conclusively: Personalized messages outpull non-personalized messages. But the word *personalized* doesn't necessarily refer to simple inclusion of the target-individual's name.

What happens when the word *dynamic* is added to personalization? It supplies a data reference for segmentation. One of the implicit benefits that e-mail has over older forms of marketing is its speed in updating an individual's value as a target.

So the term *personalization* can refer to e-mail content as well as an e-target's online or actual name. Thus, catalogs can segment their lists and personalize their e-mail offers based on their databases. Booksellers can segment their lists and personalize their offers based on the type of book an individual has bought in the past, preference for hardbound or paperback, geographical location or ZIP code, or pricing.

TIP

Be careful of overdependence on a single database factor. You can bypass eclectic tastes by catering to only one taste.

Learning a Few Rules of the Road

Rules aren't necessary if you already know a) how to write a friendly one-to-one letter and b) the primitive rules of sales.

What is a primitive rule every salesperson should know instinctively? Writing in the active voice. You're in an interactive universe, and phrases such as "Your portfolio will be evaluated" don't fly in e-mail. "We'll evaluate your portfolio" is better, and "I'll personally evaluate your portfolio" is best. You certainly know that a relationship with an individual is stronger than a relationship with an organization.

The subject line doesn't have to be short if it's pertinent to the reader. But keep that first sentence of text after the subject line short and pointed.

Much e-mail gravitates toward long paragraphs, probably out of the writer's fear that the reader will quit reading too soon. Such a writer has the logic inverted. Long paragraphs are especially deadly in e-mail.

And not only should you not be afraid to use contractions; you should use them wherever possible. It's "I'm," not "I am"; "we're," not "we are"; "you'll," not "you will." And never lapse into formal writing, such as "We shall," unless you deliberately want to be once-removed from the arena of conviviality and rapport.

Gaining Customer Retention vs. Customer Acquisition

E-mail seems to be an ideal medium for customer retention. Its combination of one-to-one, timeliness, and speed are ideal for maintaining an ongoing relationship with customers and clients . . . provided the message relates to one-to-one, timeliness, and speed.

For customer acquisition, e-mail carries the burden of an ongoing spamming image. ("Spam" is unexpected and unwanted e-mail.) Opt-in lists purchased from third parties can be both expensive and nonproductive.

Does that mean e-mail should be used for customer retention only?

Nonsense.

Rather, it means e-mail should be used with perspicacity and caution for customer acquisition. E-mail communication is less expensive than any other major medium, but effectiveness depends on the recipient agreeing that the information is valuable.

One factor that may override other considerations is that e-mail campaigns take far less time to create *and implement* than any other medium. E-mail's speed makes it the ideal medium for testing concepts, pricing, and approach.

TIP

Sending the identical message to customers and prospects is seldom an ideal communications technique. One exception that makes the conclusion valid as "seldom" instead of "never" is treating prospects as though they actually are customers. (Amateurish attempts to do this invariably result in a "spam!" accusation.)

E-mail seems to have established a permanent edge over direct mail in the battle for customer retention and in marketing almost anything to existing customers. For prospecting, the value of e-mail is cloudy because so much waste has attended early bulk-mail approaches to what is essentially a personalized medium.

Some factors when comparing e-mail to direct mail:

- Cost of the names

- Value and relevance of each name

- Relationship between the means by which the name was acquired—contest, sweepstakes, space ads, newsletter, or swap

Whether the cost goes up or down depends on the sharpness of the individual e-mail marketer.

Integrating Business E-Mail Into the Total Marketing Program

Visualize a hasty "fast action" communication one business executive sends to an associate. It's pointed, clear, short, and not larded with graphics.

Paralleling that approach is a sound e-mail procedure to business targets. Transmitting a sense of urgency is congruent with the core concept of business-to-business communication.

Flashy graphics would probably be superfluous, especially since many business offices automatically filter them out.

E-mail has rightfully become a major medium for business customer retention. The message recipient feels less put-upon when a suggestion for a reorder comes through e-mail instead of by telephone. E-mail is less interruptive because the individual "takes" the message when he or she feels most available, instead of exactly when the message is placed. Also, the means for reordering is available for immediate or later response.

TIP

E-mail that looks as though a business associate sent it may be the most effective marketing use of this medium. That means eschewing both heavy production and verbosity. But never forget that for maximum efficiency, send e-mail only when you can claim both relationship and relevance.

For actual lead generation, e-mail may not be a suitable replacement for space ads, trade shows, or direct mail; but for conversion of leads, it combines urgency and timeliness without being intrusive.

Revisiting Some Ancient Rules

A venerable rule of direct mail is: "Tell them what you're going to tell them. Then tell them. Then tell them what you've told them."

Redundant? Absolutely. Effective in e-mail messages? Absolutely.

This relates to the state of mind and shortened attention span of the e-mail recipient. An individual may sort through the components of a direct-mail package, flipping sheets back and forth. But the e-mail recipient reads in a *linear* pattern, seldom going back. The need for constant reminding of the deal is intensified.

The e-marketer seldom makes a mistake by reminding the target-individual of the offer throughout the message.

A worthwhile caution for any marketer: The attitude "customers are customers" can be a truism or a big mistake, but considering the medium as integral to the message is never a mistake.

How to Get Opt-Ins

Before worrying about people who opt out, first worry about how to get them to opt in—because if you don't have any names, opt-outs are an academic issue.

Where do the names come from? The three major sources are:

1. *Acquisition of online names and addresses of existing customers, clients, or inquirers.* This becomes considerably easier when tied to a *benefit* for supplying your name—entry in a sweepstakes, a first-order discount, or a subscription to a pertinent newsletter.

2. *Recruitment through media advertising, public relations and news releases, and telemarketing.* These tend to give a more solid base than names acquired through list rentals, because no matter how relevant a rented list may be, it's comparatively deficient in preconceived loyalty. (Make that "loyalty" in quotation marks, because the word no longer has the emotional overtones it had a couple of generations ago.)

3. *Rented names from list brokers.*

TIP

If you send news releases to media, be sure that the media regard them as *news*. Don't claim your speculations are facts because editors are wise to "vaporware" announcements. Candor goes a long way. Avoid adjectival superlatives that turn your release into a transparent piece of advertising. The acceptance rate will go up if your news actually *is* news.

Gather the Names!

Do you operate a retail store? Instruct your salespeople to ask each customer, "Do you have an online address? We'll be able to e-mail you advance notice of private sales."

Does your company take telephone orders? Be sure to include a space for your telephone representatives to ask, "Do you have an online address? We can e-mail confirmation and also let you know about specials."

Does your company enclose an order form? It should ask for an e-mail address "so we can confirm shipping date and let you know about private offers."

Does your company use a registration form? It should ask for an e-mail address "so we can contact you about upgrades."

Those examples admittedly are simplistic. Adding an incentive makes them sure-fire. The easiest incentive is promising (and delivering) a minor discount on the next order, whether in the store, over the telephone, by mail, or online.

How about free shipping as an incentive? It's powerful, all right, but it's dangerous if misused. Some e-marketers who also operate within the catalog and mail-order world blithely offer free shipping for *online sales* . . . not only cannibalizing their other revenue streams but generating resentment among customers who feel they are being penalized for preferring traditional means of ordering. It parallels the airline companies that charge a penalty for a printed ticket against an e-ticket. Ill will is as common as goodwill.

Content Is King

The dangerous marriage of arrogance and greed drove many early e-marketers to believe the raw announcement of a sweepstakes or a racy newsletter or a freebie would guarantee opt-ins.

And so it did.

But then it spurred a parallel avalanche of opt-outs once the golden glow of novelty wore off, especially for e-mails loaded with sales pitches that had no relationship to the individual demographic. The typical twenty-first century reader wants to save money and time or—which is more difficult—acquire a source of useful information. The expectation of saving money or time, or even gaining useful information, results in an opt-in. Disappointment results in an opt-out.

Club Med e-mailed a sweepstakes offer to its own database and lists of names paralleling its database. The e-mail included a survey (a response suppressor but valuable for database information) and offered a free vacation at a Club Med site as a prize. As an experiment, the e-mail also went to handheld devices.

TIP

E-mail to a handheld device has to be terse and pointed. Otherwise, not only opt-outs but also negative word-of-mouth will be fierce. As short as attention spans are on the Web, they're leisurely compared with the same person's attention span on a Palm Pilot.

Was renting lists for this sweepstakes a logical marketing investment? The answer depends almost entirely on the cost of the list, because unlike direct mail, the production cost of e-mail is negligible. So experimentation-economics are glued to the cost of names rather than the cost of production and mailing.

Figure 3-1 is a freebie offer from The American Homeowners Association. Seems official, but does such an organization actually exist? The purpose may have been to put a veneer of legitimacy on the offer because of the rampant skepticism that suppresses response.

Figure 3-1. Tell me where to send your free radio.

Subj:	**Tell me where to send your free Breeze Radio**
Date:	5:26:53 PM Pacific Standard Time
From:	AmericanHomeownersAssoc@smartreminders.com
	(American Homeowners Association)
Reply-to:	smartreminders-bounces@bounces1.smartbounce.com
To:	hglewis1@aol.com (Herschell Lewis)

Dear Herschell,

I have a brand new AM/FM Breeze Radio from the American Homeowners Association. But I need to know where to send it.

Please complete the form at the link below now so I can ship it to you immediately. Click here.

Plus, you can try our Online Grocery Coupon Warehouse. Access is free. This amazing service clips thousands of money-saving grocery coupons from newspapers and magazines and mails them to shoppers who want them.

These are the very same manufacturer's coupons for the brand name grocery products you buy every week - good for cutting your grocery bill at any store that accepts coupons.

There are currently over 50,000 coupons worth more than $30,000.00 for all major store brands.

Click here now.

Richard J. Roll, President

American Homeowners Association*
"America's #1 Homeowner Organization" Since 1994
1100 Summer Street, Stamford CT 06905
Member Service Hotline 1-800-470-2AHA (1-800-470-2242)

****
We respect your privacy and are a Certified Participant of the BBBOnLine® Privacy
Program. To be removed from future offers,please click here.

SmartReminders.com is a permission based service. To unsubscribe click here.

Does the potential of a free radio spur the typical recipient to
"Click here"? Probably, even if the radio is a tiny one from a premium
house. The word *free* still has some magic. This offer shows legitimacy by revealing two specifics that many similar offers omit—a
street address and signature to the Better Business Bureau's opt-out
availability.

Remember that content is king. And the key to coronation
is testing because of that defining phrase: *individual demographic.*

TIP

Don't offer big prizes for opt-ins. For every legitimate opt-in, you can have a
dozen freebie-hunters who have no interest other than acquiring something for
nothing. Viral mail becomes a curse rather than a blessing when an opt-in offer
is overly generous.

Double Opt-Ins

Some e-marketers, who fear being smeared with the spam accusation, have adopted a so-called double opt-in procedure. In such a

circumstance, the marketer sends an e-mail confirming the individual's willingness to accept e-mails. The individual then reconfirms.

Overkill? Wasteful? An unnecessary invitation to opt out? Astute marketers think so. The general manager of a leading e-marketing company stated flatly that he had seen no improvement in response from double opt-ins compared with the standard single opt-ins.

E-Newsletters

E-newsletters not only can "house" a multiplicity of offers—some paid for by other marketers—but also can act as a driver to the Web site. If you want to use your newsletter as a carrier rather than as a primary marketing tool, use teaser-copy and immediately highlight a link to the spot on your site instead of giving complete information about a development or a sweepstakes or a discount offer.

TIP

WARNING: You can suppress response even more easily than you might increase it.

One red flag is the current glut of e-newsletters. Tens of thousands of newsletters exist on the Web. Yes, that number includes many vertical-interest newsletters that never intend to reach broad circulation. But few online visitors regard newsletters as a novelty.

A pertinent comment came from the vice president of marketing for Forbes.com, "As long as readers feel the content is worthwhile, they will continue to subscribe." At that same time, Forbes announced a plan to expand from six e-newsletters to thirty, underlining both the value of vertical targeting as assurance against opt-outs and the increasing competition for online subscribers.

Chapter 13 discusses ways to avoid opt-outs. Part of that discussion is the optimal frequency of newsletter issuance—a delicate and crucial matter that must consider not only recipient-fatigue but also ongoing creative development.

One experiment in reducing e-newsletter opt-outs was conducted by Rising Tide Studios, a New York publisher of a free e-newsletter called *Silicon Valley Daily*. Rising Tide sent a message to about 43,000 subscribers, notifying them that if they wanted to continue receiving the newsletter free, they had to agree to opt in for a promotional weekly e-mail. Otherwise, opting out of the promotional e-mail automatically also opted them out of the newsletter . . . which itself carries banners, paid news releases, and classified advertising.

A key question in a 2001 survey to publishers cosponsored by the consulting company Clientize and the magazine *Folio* was, "Which business objective is most important to your e-newsletter?" Of those who replied, "Drive traffic to Web site" scored 36 percent; "Generate ancillary revenue" scored 32 percent; "Generate subscription sales for print brand" scored 16 percent; "Increase customer loyalty" scored 9 percent; and "Build e-mail subscriber database" scored 7 percent. "Build your Internet brand" scored zero. Note that these results applied to e-newsletters produced by those already in the publishing business.

TIP

Content is more important than production in any newsletter, whether printed or e-mailed. The first item should be a startler.

E-newsletters produced in HTML almost universally also make available a plain text version as well as one for America Online. As of this writing, the majority of e-newsletters are pure text, making it possible for almost anyone with a workable idea to produce one. The benefit is universal capability of reading the newsletter; the detriment is sameness of appearance, deadly in a fingertip-on-mouse environment. (Proponents of HTML newsletters claim HTML not only generates a substantially higher click-through rate than text but also commands more reading time.)

Some list companies offer (and often recommend) e-mail newsletter sponsorships as opposed to straight list rentals. An opt-in e-mail newsletter sponsorship is an advertisement sandwiched into the e-newsletter, which has been created and placed by someone else.

Figure 3-2 show a typical e-mail list offer sent via e-mail to marketers:

Figure 3-2. Opt-in seniors.

Marketers can reach more than 1.5 million Americans over age 50 who opted in to receive various online advertisements and promotions at their home e-mail addresses. Ninety percent of senior citizens who use the Internet also enter contests and sweepstakes. Those listed are affluent—half of them have investment portfolios that exceed $100,000, and 45% earn more than $75,000 per year. Seventy-five percent are college-educated.

The list also includes 908,574 seniors who travel. It came to market June 11.

Cost: $200/M
Selections: Age, income, gender, homeowners, new movers, grandparents, investors, bank card holders, premium card holders, cruise travelers, postal address, mail-order book/magazine/electronic product buyers, mail-order buyers with health and fitness interest, retail shoppers by type of store, state/SCF/ZIP/ZIP+4

Contact: Focus USA, Hackensack, NJ, 201-489-2525

One major list company, Worldata of Boca Raton, Florida, said in a mailed sales piece:

With the ever-present concerns over spam, Email Newsletter Sponsorships offer the benefits of permission-based Opt-In protection. The even better news is that they do so at a much *lower cost than traditional Opt-In lists. Whereas Email lists, with transmission services, typically range in price from $175/M to $300/M. Sponsorships, on the other hand, are available at a much lower cost, typically ranging in price from $10/M to $65/M.*

Well, yes, but the two aren't parallel. Yes, of course the newsletter has a benefit: Individuals have opted into it. The two detriments are: The sponsor seldom commands sole advertising attention; and the sponsor's message always, always is secondary.

The price differential certainly makes sponsorship—where available and a demographic match—a logical test.

Sweepstakes

Sweepstakes are a pain in the neck (or other parts of the anatomy). They also can bring opt-in names at a rate that leaves other methods lagging far behind.

How solid are sweepstakes names? Those who use sweepstakes almost unanimously claim that sweepstakes names respond to e-mail offers at a rate considerably higher than rented names, the claims of spam to e-mails are dramatically lower, and objections to frequent e-mails are no higher than might be expected from multi-buyers.

Jupiter Research reported in 2001 that about half (actually, 49 percent) of consumers enter an online sweepstakes at least once every month. A more significant statistic: Nearly one of every three users say they made his or her first transaction with an online marketer as the result of a promotion.

TIP

Don't limit a sweepstakes to new names because doing that can outrage the best names on any list—your active customers.

A sweepstakes can be your golden opportunity to know who is and who isn't your potential customer. With this format you have the right to ask questions individuals usually might regard as intrusive. Choose those questions carefully, because a lengthy list of questions will kill off many an otherwise enthusiastic participant.

Figure 3-3 is a typical sweepstakes invitation. Note the wording of "Please confirm your entry," suggesting that the person getting the e-mail initiated the action. Veteran Web visitors recognize this as what it is—an unsolicited attempt to gather information. Many will say, "So what? Replying costs me nothing, and I may win a personal computer."

Figure 3-3. Confirm your giveaway entry.

Subj:	**Bxtyflx, Re:Travel Winner**
Date:	4/24 5:10:25 PM Pacific Daylight Time
From:	TravelWinnings-vt@msn.com

Please confirm your entry in the Pentium 1
Gigahertz PC Giveaway within 24 hours.
Unclaimed prizes will be awarded to runners-up.

Click on the confirmation number below for details:
http://ww2.linkprizes.com/travelr/default.htm
Confirm- #748HJ8493

Thanks,
Coordinator
Brenda Johnson

Figure 3-4 is what the target-individual sees after clicking on the "Confirm" line in Figure 3-3. As you can see, the wording is careful: "You've qualified for a chance to win" and "Once registered you immediately qualify for discount vacation packages." Opt-out options should be clearly stated and not hidden, but the information demanded is formidable—home telephone, work telephone, e-mail address, age, marital status, spouse's name, and even family income. This is information the marketer could never hope to get without an artificial incentive.

Figure 3-4. You are qualified to win.

Congratulations you've qualified
for a chance to win one of the exclusive
Vacation Packages below
This is the real thing.
Simply fill out the form below
and register to win-*5 drawings weekly*.

Confirm Entry Below

Register for your dream vacation here. Once registered you immediately qualify for highly discounted vacation packages! Up to 70%! You Can't Lose Either Way!

What happens is the transmission of an enormous amount of marketable information. In essence, a trade has taken place: The mailer trades a prize of nominal worth for information that, in a compiled list, can be used to e-mail that person repeatedly, avoiding the spam accusation by pointing out the relationship.

Figure 3-5 and Figure 3-6 are additional examples of the something-for-nothing technique used to recruit opt-in names. Note the careful wording of Figure 3-5, which suggests the recipient had entered "something" and is a winner. The intent, a common opt-in method, is to gather names. Also, note the signature by an individual.

Figure 3-5. Your registration is confirmed.

Subj:	**Re: Registration Confirmation 4**
Date:	6:20:45 PM Pacific Standard Time
From:	connieconi@earthlink.net
To:	hglewis1@aol.com

Confirm registration code
for your winning entry
http://www.travelplansusa.com_please_review_the_details_of_the_pentium_pc_gi
veaway_at_your_earliest_possible_convenience.winning-travel-
entry.com@www.netfreewebsite.org/vac/
Entry Confirmation #LKIR45YT

Wishing you a fun filled vacation.

If you should have any additional
questions do not hesitate to contact
me direct.

Kelly Meyer
Account Coordinator
National Vacation Promotions

There is something of a paradox in Figure 3-6. The unsolicited message claims to represent an opportunity to "take back your mailbox," while qualifying for a $100,000 giveaway. As an incentive, entrants receive $500 worth of shopping coupons.

TIP

To add verisimilitude and credibility to an e-mail offer that may strain credulity, include the signature of what appears to be a representative of the sender.

Figure 3-6. Take back your mailbox.

Subj:	**$100,000 Give Away III**
Date:	8:10:01 PM Pacific Standard Time
From:	traffix@response.etracks.com (Traffix)
To:	hglewis1@aol.com

hglewis1@aol.com:

This is your lucky day!
RightOffers.com provides you with the opportunity to reduce junk mail and receive only the offers you want. Click the link below, complete the brief survey, and AUTOMATICALLY receive $500 worth of FREE shopping coupons, plus the chance to win the $100,000 Give Away III !!

Click here!

Take back your mailbox and receive an automatic entry into the $100,000 Give Away III, just for filling out the online survey.
This offer is brought to you by Traffix in association with RightOffers.com.
If you do not wish to receive future RightOffers promotions from Traffix, click here to unsubscribe.

The question always concerns the worth of names harvested through unsolicited free offers. A logical marketing move is an ongoing "winner update"—a reason to send e-mails. Eventually, when winners are announced, try to make everyone a winner by issuing an online discount coupon. But merely announcing, "You've won a discount," in no way is as emotionally satisfying as an actual printable coupon. Numbering the coupon ties it to a potential online transaction.

Robert Dunhill, of Dunhill International List Company, made this statement in a published paper about e-mail lists: "Those who participate in online contests are generally willing to exchange a certain level of personal information for the chance to win a prize of perceived personal value."

It's a swap. In any trade, equivalence is the key to mutual satisfaction. What does the sweepstakes operator get in exchange for making prizes available? Information ranges from raw online names (of dubious worth) to substantial demographic/psychographic background that enables message tailoring. Obviously, the more information one demands, the greater the number of people who drop off without supplying information. Is it a worthwhile trade? Probably, but only testing can answer that question.

Are you worried because so many people are semiprofessional contest entrants, available to you only because they want something for nothing? The answer to that question is easy: If this common attitude worries you, don't have a sweepstakes.

TIP

The bigger the grand prize, the greater the extended time before the drawing can be. To keep the pot boiling, allow additional entries for additional action or purchases.

"We Want Your Opinion"

Media have led the way in capturing e-mail addresses by saying, "We want your opinion." Responders log onto a Web site and give their opinions about controversial matters.

For local communities, such matters might be elections, taxes, a current courtroom trial, architecture, a movie, a television show, or a celebrity. For a business, such matters might be good/bad idea, new use, opinion of an upgrade or new model, response to an offer, government regulation or intervention, or monetary value.

In each case, quoting some of the responses in e-mails to the participating universe will make the respondents whom you quote your friends for life. Others will be more inclined to participate in the next "We want your opinion."

Even simpler is asking for an online vote. People typically vote yes or no . . . accompanied by their online addresses.

Acknowledging the vote establishes an e-mail relationship, and if you accompany the thank-you acknowledgment with a special offer, that offer can't be regarded as spam. You also have free second and third shots, because you can report the percentile results in an e-mail message, then contact the list again asking for another vote. (The typical time gap is two weeks.)

Permissioned Lists

Lists exist of individuals who have indicated willingness to receive e-mail from outside sources. How valid are these lists as sources of e-mail response?

The only way to determine whether a specific list works for your specific type of offer is to rent some names. How many? Most analysts recommend a minimum of ten thousand.

A rented list is the chimera, the question mark, the third rail on which e-marketers stagger. The cost of rented names was double or triple the cost of similar names rented for direct mail, until two problems seemed to develop in 2001—a name-glut and the realization that there was a high opt-out rate for rented names.

At this writing, the cost of renting e-mail permissioned list names is still higher than direct mail lists at fifteen to twenty-five cents each, which is considerably more expensive than the same names would cost for a direct-mail campaign . . . but then, the cost of reaching these people by e-mail is far lower than the cost of reaching them by direct mail.

That brings up an interesting speculation: Why not rent the same names for less money, for a direct postcard? The postcard includes "an offer you can't refuse" for visiting a particular Web site. The Web site then has the offer, requiring e-mail registration for participation.

Or follow the newest trend of integrated marketing, which includes an actual name and address along with the e-mail name, so a marketer can double-attack a prospect.

Is it worth trying? Certainly.

When renting lists, an absolute demand any e-marketer should make is a guarantee that the names are indeed opt-ins. Under optimum conditions, the list broker should agree to replace names that immediately opt out. (Optimum conditions seldom exist.)

TIP

Don't drive direct-mail leads to your home page if you want to capture the e-mail address. Send them to a URL that displays an immediate, clear, and irresistible offer. After all, by establishing a detour to the home page, you're actually in a three-step conversion.

When renting lists from several sources or several lists from the same source, the "merge-purge" provision should apply: A computer program eliminates duplications. Thus, someone whose name appears on two sweepstakes lists, or on a newsletter list and a buyer list, will receive only one e-mail.

Complicating any merge-purge or analysis is the tendency of many Web visitors to use a multiplicity of online names. Some rented lists perform poorly because of a situation peculiar to the Internet and never before experienced in mass media: A high number of individuals reserve an online name for free offers. They not only don't buy through that name, they aggressively avoid buying. Having that name on a list, especially a list compiled from a free offer, can be deadly. This is one reason to test a list before jumping in with both feet.

Historically, the direct-mail industry prefers buyers over newsletters or sweepstakes entrants, because these individuals have demonstrated a willingness to spend—the ultimate indication of interaction—and not just be passive recipients. Quite logically, buyer names are usually more expensive than sweepstakes or newsletter names.

One important qualifier: Be sure to purge from any rented list the names of individuals who have opted out of your house list. This requires electronic software every list source should have available.

Third-Party Endorsements

Third-party endorsements are finding their way into the e-mail universe.

Suppose I sell computer hardware and software and you sell office furniture. Instead of my e-mailing your names on a list-swap, the e-mail to your list comes from *you*. The benefit is obvious: E-mail comes from a known source instead of an unknown source.

Your e-mail message would point out that because of the friendship between your company and mine, you have negotiated to have this offer extended to your preferred customers on the same basis as my company is offering it to our own preferred customers. Then a link brings the individual to the proper page on my Web site. I reciprocate in e-mail to my customers.

TIP

For verisimilitude, do not link to the other company's home page. Link to a page with the "special offer" mentioned in the e-mail.

Levels of Opting In

The basic e-mail option, both standard and dull in Web sites and media advertising, is worded something like this:

Please check this box if you would like to be notified by e-mail of products or services that may be of interest to you.

Unquestionably, the statement represents an absolute opt-in. The individual is required to check the box, asking for e-mail.

A more targeted option, and the choice of those who prefer selective names to mass names, is an opt-in invitation worded something like this:

> *Want to be kept up-to-date on new offers and specials? Just click here and we'll put you on our preferred list.*

Note the two motivators built into this latter opt-in—exclusivity and greed. Those who employ this type of wording report a bonus: a lower eventual percentage of opt-outs, possibly because a touch of guilt is added to the motivational mix.

A third approach is the negative-option technique, which picks up names without a positive action on the part of the individual:

> *Occasionally, we may send you information from a select group of vendors about products in which you probably are interested. If you prefer to not have such information, click here.*

In this instance, the individual has to perform a positive act to *not* get the e-mail.

Then we have the "hook" opt-in, which ties a person's primary benefit to an automatic agreement:

> *Along with your subscription, you have agreed to receive special announcements. These help us provide the service you want and also help you by making available offers you otherwise might not see.*

No "click here" to validate this option. It becomes part of an agreed transaction. (Later on, especially if the company is a member of The Direct Marketing Association, each e-mail will include an opt-out option.)

Is There a Difference?

Critics complain—often without evidence—that automatic opt-ins produce poorer names than deliberate opt-ins.

Buying histories tend to discredit such complaints. Yes, some sweepstakes entrants respond only to "something for nothing" offers. That pattern isn't new; it's as old as media and mailed contests themselves.

E-marketers, just as retail advertisers in conventional media, depend on percentages. That same individual who sits on a list, clicking and deleting message after message, suddenly responds. Why? Because suddenly a specific message hits a specific hot button.

The challenge for marketers is to mount as dynamic a series of offers as the marketplace allows. Until an individual clicks "Let me out," the proper assumption is that a buyer lurks behind the fingertip.

Avoiding the "Spam" Accusation

Spam was a product of World War II, available to troops in the field and to civilians through grocery stores. How many other items that were on store shelves sixty years ago still survive?

The original Spam was and is a canned meat product consisting primarily of chopped pork that is pressed into a loaf. The twenty-first century spam is about as pejorative a term as anyone can apply to e-mail. Spam's new definition refers to sending numerous copies of the same message *to people who aren't expecting to hear from you.*

Note the italicized wording. It isn't to people who aren't expecting *that message*; it's to people who aren't expecting to hear *from you.*

Big difference!

Tens of millions of words have appeared in print, attacking or defending a marketer's right to send unexpected e-mail. Lawsuits have been filed. With the proliferation of e-mail marketers (the most natural marketing evolution in the last two hundred years) and the increasing sophistication of list segmenting and database dependence, the battle can only intensify.

Robert Dunhill of Dunhill International List Company points out: "Opt-in e-mail is not spam. Spam is unsolicited e-mail, whereas opt-in e-mail is requested by a subscriber based on a value proposition to fulfill a specified need or desire."

Early Internet historians often credit the term *spam*, as it applies to the World Wide Web, to an old Monty Python sketch in which a gaggle of Vikings sit in a café that serves only Spam and sing, "Spam spam spam spam, lovely spam."

Who Are the Culprits?

The entire concept of spam stems from e-mail's early days, when sending e-mails paralleled the Wild West of pioneer times. The medium was both unregulated and untested, and marketers picked up names everywhere, including chatrooms, surreptitiously swapped lists, and communications never intended to be on file. Offers were as loose and unrelenting as a carnival pitch.

The result? Consumer complaints became a tidal wave, to the extent that some critics and commentators labeled every commercial message spam. Thus, permission marketing was born and quickly became the battle cry.

Spam is a derogatory term than eventually may fade into disuse, because many of the bandits have left the arena and others have switched to a more contemporary marketing attitude. The Direct Marketing Association insists that any member adhere to the principles of permission marketing—getting the prospective recipient's permission before sending an e-mail message.

The ancient marketing trick of stating that the message was recommended by a friend has become epidemic on the Web. The examples in Figure 4-1 and Figure 4-2 (only the beginnings are reprinted here) are actual and typical. But are they spam?

Figure 4-1. Message from a friend.

Subj:	John thought you might like this. 1085012
Date:	8/29/ 10:07:05 PM Eastern Daylight Time
To:	[I've deleted a huge group of online names]

Best Life Insurance, Lowest Cost!

You could save 90% on Life Insurance!

CLICK HERE NOW FOR A FREE REAL-TIME QUOTE

Three days later, this message is sent:

Figure 4-2. Hello again.

Subj:	**Sue thought you might like this 1167773**
Date:	9/1/ 7:31:09 AM Eastern Daylight Time
From:	an1arturobelinda@msn.com (an1arturobelinda@msn.com)
To:	[Again I've deleted a huge group of online names]

The Best Life Insurance, Lowest Cost!

Shop, Compare and Save
Save up to 80% on your current term life insurance

**Comparing the best values from among hundreds of the nation's top insur-
ance companies!**

Fill out the simple form, and you'll have the
15 best custom quotes in under 1 minute.
1 answer a few questions
2 receive the 15 lowest quotes
3 choose a policy and apply online

(continues)

Figure 4-2. (*continued*)

Compare rates from hundreds of companies INSTANTLY

Click Here to Compare!

Not only are these e-mails spam, but they're the cause of a negative reaction bleeding over onto all commercial e-mail messages. Similar to these messages is the tactic of using, "Bob thought you might like this," as reprinted in Chapter 5 (Figure 5-2).

Activists have accused most of the major Web e-mail services of sending spam—Microsoft's Hotmail, the Yahoo! mail service, porn vendors, and innumerable one-shot e-marketers who pitch everything from loans and investments to books and records. One group of activists claimed that Hotmail played into the hands of spammers by sending online addresses to an online directory operated by Infospace, Inc., where they could become available to anyone who wants to send spam. (The anti-spammers tend to counter spam by using a process called "dictionary attack"—overloading the suspect's e-mail address with addresses randomly generated by computers, a technique parallel to random-digit dialing of telephone numbers.)

Hotmail rejected the spam accusation by saying it had revised its Web pages to prevent visibility of users' e-mail addresses.

Is It Only Spam in the Eye of the Beholder?

No clear definition of spam can exist, because spam is in the eye of the beholder: One person's spam is another person's salvation.

An example is Figure 4-3, which will annoy some and be greeted with enthusiasm by others. As e-mailer databases become more specific, the disparity may never diminish. Why? Because inevitably some individuals welcome announcements of products and services aimed at their demographic/psychographic profiles, while others regard such information as breaking and entering their private domains.

The message in Figure 4-3, which is reprinted in full, typifies those offers that are out in left field. Few people will regard it as spam, because few people would expect to be accosted by such a proposition. That it is unsolicited advertising is unquestioned. Phrases such as "order form" and "all orders filled within twenty-four hours of receiving them" make it clear that this is a commercial message.

(*text continues on page 61*)

Figure 4-3. Out in left field.

Subj:	**FYI**
Date:	4/13 4:44:10 PM Pacific Daylight Time
From:	jjizc@bluemail.dk
To:	174@mailasia.com

Minister Charles Simpson has the power to make you a LEGALLY ORDAINED MINISTER within 48 hours!!!!   l2x

BE ORDAINED NOW!

As a minister, you will be authorized to perform the rites and ceremonies of the church!!

WEDDINGS
MARRY your BROTHER, SISTER, or your BEST FRIEND!!
Don't settle for being the BEST MAN OR BRIDES' MAID
Most states require that you register your certificate
(THAT WE SEND YOU) with the state prior to conducting the ceremony.

FUNERALS
A very hard time for you and your family
Don't settle for a minister you don't know!!
Most states require that you register your certificate

(*continues*)

Figure 4-3. (*continued*)

(THAT WE SEND YOU) with the state prior to conducting the ceremony.

BAPTISMS
You can say "WELCOME TO THE WORLD!!!! I AM YOUR MINISTER AND YOUR UNCLE!!"
What a special way to welcome a child of God.

FORGIVENESS OF SINS
The Catholic Church has practiced the forgiveness of sins for centuries
**Forgiveness of Sins is granted to all who ask in sincerity and willingness to change for the better!!

VISIT CORRECTIONAL FACILITIES
Since you will be a Certified Minister, you can visit others in need!!
Preach the Word of God to those who have strayed from the flock

WANT TO START YOUR OWN CHURCH??
After your LEGAL ORDINATION, you may start your own congregation!!

At this point you must be wondering how much the Certificate costs. Right?
Well, let's talk about how much the program is worth. Considering the value of becoming a CERTIFIED MINISTER I'd say the program is easily worth $100.
Wouldn't you agree? However, it won't cost that much. Not even close! My goal is to make this life changing program affordable so average folks can benefit from the power of it.

Since I know how much you want to help others, you're going to receive your Minister Certification for under $100.00... Not even $50.00... You are going to receive the entire life-changing course for only $29.95.
For only $29.95 you will receive:
1. 8-inch by 10-inch certificate IN COLOR, WITH GOLD SEAL.
(CERTIFICATE IS PROFESSIONALLY PRINTED BY AN INK PRESS)
2. Proof of Minister Certification in YOUR NAME!!
3. SHIPPING IS FREE!!!

****

LIMITED TIME OFFER: ORDER TODAY!
SEND Only $29.95 US
(CREDIT CARD, CASH, CHECK, OR MONEY ORDER)
SHIPPING IS FREE!!! For Shipping OUTSIDE the US please add $11.00.

To place your order merely fill out the following form and fax to 1-775-640-6547.
If this line is busy, please try faxing to 1-208-694-2787.

or mail to:

Internet Information Services
PO Box 21442
Billings, MT 59104

(ALL ORDERS FILLED WITHIN 24 HOURS OF RECEIVING THEM)
*Please allow 8 days to receive your certificate by mail.
If you do not receive your order within 10 days, please send us a fax letting us
know of the late arrival. We will then contact you to figure out why you have not
received your order.

****
Credit Card Order Form
(Please print very clearly in dark ink)

Name on Credit Card:

Address:

City/State/ZIP:

Your email address:

Your card will be charged $29.95 for your Ministers' Certificate.
For Shipping OUTSIDE the US please add $11.00.

(continues)

Figure 4-3. (*continued*)

Type of Card, circle one (Visa, MasterCard, American Express)

Credit Card Number:

Date Credit Card Expires:

Please tell us your phone Number:

Please tell us your fax Number:

To order by Check or Money Order:

MAKE YOUR CHECK PAYABLE TO:
Internet Information Services

(Please Print Clearly Your Name and Address)

Name:

Address:

City/State/ZIP:

E-mail Address:

Please tell us your phone Number:

Please tell us your fax Number:

(ALL ORDERS FILLED WITHIN 24 HOURS OF RECEIVING THEM)
*Please allow 8 days to receive your certificate by mail.
If you do not receive your order within 10 days, please send us a fax letting us
know of the late arrival. We will then contact you to figure out why you have not
received your order.

Thank you for your business,
Internet Information Services
PO Box 21442
Billings, MT 59104

Fax to 1-775-640-6547. If this line is busy, please try faxing to 1-208-694-2787.

Copyright (c) 1997-2000
All Rights Reserved

+++
This ad is produced and sent out by:
Universal Advertising Systems
To be removed from our mailing list please email us at
vanessagreen@freeze.com with remove in the subject line or
call us toll free at 1-888-605-2485 and give us your email address
or write us at: Central DB Removal, PO Box 1200, Oranjestad, Aruba
+++

But when a message comes from an unknown source and includes an online address that apparently doesn't exist, the accusation of spam may be undeniable. Figure 4-4 is an example of this type of message.

(*text continues on page 64*)

Figure 4-4. This stock is ready to rock.

Subj:	**OTCBB : CBNK * This Stock Is Ready To Rock Today! * ...** **8/31/2001 6:21:13 PM**
Date:	8/31 7:21:51 PM Eastern Daylight Time
From:	dbussm8000@yahoo.com
CC:	lesli0730@aol.com, branda68219@aol.com, sweetreat1@aol.com, sciolli@aol.com, kevl211@aol.com, csanovafly@aol.com, milka43@aol.com, speedy9556@aol.com, bfettxx@aol.com, markbramm@aol.com, speedy968@aol.com, speedy9684@aol.com, aqueous55@aol.com, nick4everhr@aol.com, upops@aol.com

(continues)

Figure 4-4. (*continued*)

Dear Friend,

You are recieving this E-mail because you were referred, if you wish to be removed simply click reply and you will be removed immediately. If you are not interested in stocks and know someone who is please forward this E-mail to them so they will love you forever :)

Company: Custom Branded Networks
Symbol: OTCBB: CBNK
Authorized: 100,000,000
Issued & Outstanding: 40,000,000
Restricted: 25,000,000
Float: 15,000,000

Custom Branded Networks (CBNK) is a leader in providing 100% turnkey Private Label Internet Services, focusing on three core business models - private-label and direct ISP services, Internet service software, and direct response sales. Focusing on these three business models generates a predictable and consistent revenue stream for the Company.

Organizations such as churches, schools and small businesses now have the opportunity to earn additional revenue or raise money through the leveraging of their existing membership. CBNK's proprietary software and strategic alliances with companies like Quest Communications, offers organizations with as few as 100 members the ability to provide custom branded ISP services. By partnering with organizations, CBNK eliminates the cost to market its ISP services to the end user, maximizing profit potential and allowing it to pass those savings onto its clients.
On August 14, 2001, CBNK announced that it had reached an agreement to acquire UsefulWare, Inc., a leading provider of signup software for ISP's. The deal was made for an undisclosed sum of cash and stock. Under the agreement, UsefulWare will continue to operate as a separate business unit and wholly owned subsidiary of CBNK. Driven by the needs of ISPs, and other Internet businesses, UsefulWare offers a full line of products and services for making the experience of new Internet users an easy and productive one.

As a business-to-business (B2B) supplier, UsefulWare works behind the scenes with some of the largest and most well known names in the Internet business world including AOL and AT&T. UsefulWare complements CBNK's software with a full line of back office services. The Company has been in business for 5 years, is debt free and in its last fiscal year had revenues in excess of $1.4 Million and approximately 300 active customers representing 900,000 ISP subscribers.

CBNK has established a strategic alliance with One4Luck to develop a direct response sales program. One4Luck will work with CBNK to produce and air a 30 minute infomercial offering the Company's custom brandable ISP services in conjunction with other Internet services including on-line brokerage, banking and other financial services. One4Luck has had tremendous success with its "Teach Me To Trade" infomercial with has sold over 50,000 units since airing in the fall of 2000.

Through these core business units, CBNK anticipates revenue in excess $3 Million. Additional acquisitions are currently being negotiated and the Company intends to continue an aggressive growth strategy.

Investor Relations:

(877) 609-0442 toll free

Disclaimer: Certain statements in this document are "forward-looking statements" as outlined in the Private Securities Litigation Act of 1995 within the meanings of Section 27A of the Securities Act and Section 21E of the Exchange Act and are subject to certain risks and uncertainties. These risks and uncertainties include but are not limited to economic conditions, changes in the law or regulations, demand for products and services of the company, in the effects of competition. These risks and uncertainties could significantly affect results in the future and actual results may differ materially form any representations herein. Forward-looking statements are typically identified by the words: believe, expect, anticipate, intend, estimate, and similar expressions or which by there nature refer to future events. This editorial shall not constitute an offer to sell any securities or solicitation of an offer to buy any securities. This publication is an advertisement on behalf of the said company and may not

(continues)

Figure 4-4. (*continued*)

> be construed as investment advice. This is not to be purported to be a complete analysis of the company mentioned. Investing in securities is speculative and carries a high degree of risk. Past performance does not guarantee future results. Readers should consult with there own independent tax; business and financial advisors with respect to any investment, including any contemplated investment in the advertised company. All information contained in this advertisement should be independently verified with the advertised company and any independent financial analyst. The reader and/or viewer should independently investigate and fully understand all risks. The company has pursuant to a written agreement, with F Web Corp., that provided for the immediate payment of 5,000 cash for its services which includes but is not limited to; printed, audio, video and electronic dissemination of information concerning the profiled company and the streaming video & audio interviews of the company management. F Web Corp. has not received any other compensation, of any kind, for this promotion. Web Corp. is not a registered investment advisor or a broker dealer.

The nature of the communication in Figure 4-4, referred to as stock "touting," suggests spam. Evidence that the accusation may be correct is in Figure 4-5, a reply asking to be removed from the list. (Note terms such as *leader* and *predictable* and *consistent revenue stream* in the first paragraph of text and the disclaimer at the end of the text in Figure 4-4.)

Figure 4-5 is the result of the recipient's attempt to remove her name from such communications.

Figure 4-5. Service unavailable.

Subj:	**Returned mail: Service unavailable**
Date:	9/1/ 7:02:07 AM Eastern Daylight Time
From:	MAILER-DAEMON@aol.com (Mail Delivery Subsystem)
To:	Demonelle@aol.com

The original message was received at Sat, 1 Sep 07:01:52 -0400 (EDT) from root@localhost

—— The following addresses had permanent fatal errors ——
<dbussm8000@yahoo.com>

—— Transcript of session follows ——
... while talking to mx2.mail.yahoo.com.:
>>> DATA
<<< 554 delivery error: dd This user doesn't have a yahoo.com account
(dbussm8000@yahoo.com) - mta454.mail.yahoo.com
554 <dbussm8000@yahoo.com>... Service unavailable

Pros and Cons of Rented Lists

In the early burst of enthusiasm over e-mail, list companies were charging two to three times as much to rent online names as they charged for names to be sent via conventional mail.

Several problems pertained. (I'm putting this discussion in the past tense because as e-mail list rentals mature, many negative circumstances no longer exist.) One was the origin of the names.

Many names—in some cases, the majority of them—were individuals who traded their names for something free. Whether a newsletter, a "Joke of the Day," a sample sent for shipping cost only, or a sweepstake, these names were not optimal as potential buyers.

Online names that did not include actual names and addresses were more suspect, because they were impenetrable and, in some cases, phony.

Another problem has been the rawness of the names. Many lists include no specifics for targeting.

And merge-purge, that venerable technique of avoiding duplication, has been a difficult process in e-mail list comparisons. The lack of merge-purge when testing lists can result in multiple submissions to individuals, which is an invitation for a spam accusation.

In e-mail, as in conventional direct response, growth of the buyer universe has to come from the outside, whether through recommendations or through solicitations. Refinement of lists, more specific profiling, and flexibility of list formatting can be a major key for many e-marketers.

Who Are the Protectors?

The late Jimmy Durante had a memorable line: "Everybody wants to get into the act."

From state attorneys general to members of the U.S. Congress to local politicians to editorial writers to trade associations, outcry against spam is constant. After all, spam is an easy target.

Within the supplier community, a group of fifteen companies has formed The Responsible Electronic Communications Alliance. At an industry trade show, this alliance offered a four-point proposal for e-marketers. The proposal, as outlined in a news release:

1. Bans advertisers from sending solicitations to consumers without consent.

2. Allows consumers to remove themselves from mailing lists.

3. Restricts e-mail to relevant content.

4. Requires members to state how the information customers provide will be used.

Obviously, if all e-marketers observed all four points of the proposal, spam would cease to exist, except as a historical curiosity. That third point is one that requires knowledge of demographic/psychographic profiles, which could be the worthwhile underpinning of this concept. It also could be a catch-22, because the only way to achieve relevant content is to compile demographic/psychographic information beforehand. At press time, the proposal was still just that—a proposal.

Is Spamming a Genuine Threat?

With each passing year, reaction to spam (or messages that might be spam) seems to be milder. One reason might be that the practice itself has been downgraded from infuriation to annoyance.

The Direct Marketing Association requires its members to include an opt-out capability for each e-mail message. Once an individual has opted out, that sender no longer can include *or* swap his or her name, which gradually cleans the potential universe. A company in Franklin, Ohio, called Removeyou.com is the source of a so-called "live" list of the Internet addresses of people who have asked to be removed from bulk e-mail lists. Removeyou.com contacts companies that were accused of spamming and invites them to participate; those who do send their lists to Removeyou.com, which removes the online addresses of those who have registered the desire to be excluded from unsolicited e-mail.

Why should a company cooperate with the Direct Marketing Association or participate with Removeyou.com? One reason is to head off legislation that might damage legitimate e-mail along with borderline or illegitimate e-mail.

There are many individuals who welcome messages from anyone—including unsolicited mail offers. Over time, unquestionably e-mail lists compiled with an eye toward legitimacy will become more valid and more closely match the demographics of the message recipients. A matched message greatly reduces the possibility of being regarded as spam.

TIP

When renting e-mail lists, a key anti-spam accusation question is: "Have parallel companies e-mailed this list before, and what kind of response did they get?" Two assumptions are vital for giving value to the question and the answer to it: (1) Is the answer to your question truthful? (2) If the answer is truthful, has the list been e-mailed so heavily that the cream is out of the bottle?

E-Mail Referrals and Viral Mail: Are They Spam?

The member-get-a-member tactic is as ancient as the Doubleday Book Club. Marketers assume, quite rightly, that friends and relatives share a demographic sameness. So exploiting that sameness with rewards to all parties benefits everyone.

Without incentives, these programs seldom succeed today. Not only are the targets familiar with incentives, they expect them. But the incentives needn't be merchandise. Discount coupons benefit everybody. Additional entries in a sweepstakes cost nothing beyond simple bookkeeping entries. A sales commission on the first sale to a referred friend is dangerous because it rips the seventh veil off the "Do a special friend a special favor" approach . . . but for that very reason it may be worth testing.

TIP

Immediately acknowledge every e-mail referral with a thank-you e-mail. Equally immediate should be your contact to the referred individual. If you are not ready to do that, hold up the program until you are.

Another popular approach is asking the recipient to e-mail the message to a friend. Most Web-access companies, such as America Online, have a one-click "Forward" icon. An increasing number of Web marketers have an "E-mail this *page* to a friend" link, enabling a visitor to e-mail the page immediately. The page arrives, from the person forwarding it and not from the company whose site it represents . . . making the acceptance potential considerably greater.

Obviously, e-mail from a friend or relative is not spam. Equally obvious is the desire of some legislators to define such e-mail as spam, because of the commercial intent. Should the marketer run scared? In my opinion—and it's just that, an opinion—the answer is no. Classifying e-mail referrals as spam grossly exceeds any logical interpretation. Two cautions:

1. No amount of logic will deter a legislator who feels the need to make a point. Anyone in a business as new and hot and dynamic as e-mail marketing is subject to the peril of a legislator's ego.

2. The purpose of name acquisition is to establish an opt-in relationship, which means that follow-up communications direct from the company have to be worded with exquisite care and loaded with benefits.

Port 25 Blocking

Port 25 blocking is a term that is used to describe the gate-closing procedures of service providers that maintain open relays for e-mail to reach its intended destination. Blocking usually occurs after complaints from subscribers. Some of those complaints are simply a statement of annoyance; others are threats to flood the service providers' online servers with so many opposing e-mails that the result would be a service outage. A paradox exists here: Objections to spam manifest themselves as spam. (E-mail from members of The Direct Marketing Association always includes an opt-out, but the association cannot control non-members.)

Does the First Amendment offer protection against Port 25 blocking? Probably not. Service providers aren't federally licensed like broadcast stations. A groundswell movement against blocking would be difficult to mount, except perhaps for a consortium of e-marketers.

The accusation of spam, whether legitimate complaint or not, is as old as e-mail itself. And e-marketers represent as broad a spectrum as conventional mailers. Some are 100 percent legitimate, while some are 75 percent legitimate, some 50 percent, and some zero. In today's marketing ambience, e-mail is simply typical of the marketplace.

Anti-Spam Web Sites

Typical of the burgeoning anti-spam marketplace, which has become a surprisingly rabid and sometimes commercial enterprise on its own, are three of what seem to be thousands of anti-spam Web sites.

One is the Spam Recycling Center. This organization is a consortium of three anti-spam activist groups: ChooseYourMail.com, Forum for Responsible Ethical E-Mail (F.R.E.E.), and The Coalition Against Unsolicited Commercial E-Mail (CAUCE). According to promotional statements on its Web site, the Spam Recycling Center gives recipients a convenient and free outlet for forwarding what individuals may regard as spam to the appropriate federal authorities; get a free anti-spam filter from Brightmail, GFI, or MailCircuit; and subscribe to a newsletter.

Spam Hater is a free Windows download that lists the following services on its Web site:

- Analyzes the spam

- Extracts a list of addresses of relevant postmasters

- Prepares a reply

- Offers a choice of legal threats, insults, or your own message

- Appends a copy of the spam if required

- Puts it in a mail window ready for sending

- Provides a tool to help keep you out of spammers' databases

- Analyzes Usenet spam

- Offers context-sensitive help, by using a right mouse click on the item concerned

- Shows a sample of the spam it's analyzing

- Offers the *Whois* program to help track the perpetrator

- Generates a "TRACEROUTE" query to help track the perpetrator's upstream provider

It is easy to see how passionate some anti-spam advocates can become. Is their position rational and logical? That, obviously, depends on both the individual's reaction to online solicitation and attitude toward what *constitutes* spam.

SpamCop's home page has three major headings: (1) Sick of Spam? (2) Really Sick of Spam? and, surprisingly, (3) Reported for Spamming?

That latter heading leads to answers to the site's most common questions, such as "SpamCop got it wrong! How can I fix it? Falsely accused? What is spam? Find help here for Internet and hosting providers as well as small and large-scale bulk mailers." A click tells e-marketers what to do if they feel they have been reported falsely to SpamCop.

CAUCE describes itself this way:

CAUCE, The Coalition Against Unsolicited Commercial Email, is an ad hoc, all volunteer organization, created by Netizens to advocate for a legislative solution to the problem of UCE (a/k/a "spam").

The organization e-mails messages headed "Stop Spam on the Internet!" Typical wording is as follows:

Boycott Internet Spam!

You have probably seen an increase in the amount of "junk mail" that shows up in your e-mail box, or on your favorite newsgroup. The activities of a small number of people are becoming a bigger problem for the Internet. We have been actively engaged in fighting spam for years. Since we presented this site to the public in 1996, we have been pleased to be referenced as one of the best anti-spam sites on the net.

Help fight spam to keep the Internet useful for everyone.

Hot News: A spammer has chosen to try to tar spam.abuse.net with the same brush. We are not sending any e-mail out that links to this site. If you got a spam that does so, please send it along with full headers and we will notify the relevant abuse departments.

What is spam? | Why is it bad? | Spammers do more than spam | What not to do about spam | Frequently Asked Questions | Other Voices | Other anti-spam sites | We are not opposed to Commerce | A few suggestions on how to market on the Internet | Status on efforts to outlaw spam

Copies of this site in California, USA (original), New Jersey, USA, Australia, Austria, France (in French), France (alternate, in French), France (in English), Germany (Deutschland), Greece, Israel, Israel (alternate), Japan, Spain, The Netherlands, Turkey, and the UK are available.

Please support the effort to outlaw spam. See CAUCE for more information. The editor-in-chief and many of the signatories and contributors of and to this site are supporters of CAUCE. Join with us and lobby Congress to make spamming illegal in the United States.

One of the segments in a typical message offers specific suggestions to those who accept this philosophy:

Practical Tools to Boycott Spam

Boycott spam. Take advantage of our technical expertise by using the following tools and techniques. Look for more methods to appear here.

- Filtering mail to your personal account

- Blocking spam e-mail for an entire site

- Blocking Usenet spam for an entire site

- Blocking IP connectivity from spam sites

- Other tools and techniques for limiting spam

- Mail Abuse Prevention System (MAPS) LLC and its various automated lists, including its flagship Realtime Blackhole List (RBL).

- Sample Acceptable Use Policy statements for ISPs

- Brett Glass has put together a comprehensive paper on stopping spam on BSD UNIX systems

Organized and Unorganized E-Mail Opposition

It's not surprising that a growing number of businesses either demand that their employees not receive e-mail on the company's computers or use bulk-mail inboxes to intercept and ignore or delete e-mail messages.

E-mail providers and search engines sometimes join the anti-spam parade. Yahoo and MSN Hotmail routinely divert e-mail messages that seem to be spam into a subscriber's bulk-mail inbox, where positive attention is unlikely.

Online veterans often use fake e-mail addresses when they register at Web sites. Why? To avoid being circularized with e-mail they implicitly regard as spam.

TIP

Two of the most foolproof techniques for avoiding the spam-accusation are (1) relevance to the individual's own business or lifestyle, and (2) avoiding the appearance of having produced just another sales pitch.

Do marketers have an antitoxin? Oh, yes. The positive procedures described in this book are some of the ingredients.

Is It "Is" or Is It "Ain't"?

The ancient saying, "One man's meat is another man's poison," might well have been written for the confusing e-mail universe, in which both experts and fanatics abound.

Take a look at Figure 4-6: "A friend has sent you this NetLaughter funpage." The heading suffers because technology can only forward, not specify which friend. The sender's identity is buried in the text. But any forwarded message by a known noncommercial contact cannot be regarded as spam.

Did a friend really refer this proposition? Possibly. Note the signature, "Love, C," and what appears to be a personal reference.

Figure 4-6. An e-mail greeting from me to you.

Subj:	E-greeting from me to you!
Date:	4/30/ 6:15:18 AM Pacific Daylight Time
From:	comradp@aol.com
Sender:	apache@supertaf.com (Apache)
To:	hglewis1@aol.com

Hi,

A friend has sent you this NetLaughter funpage/greeting!
Go here to see it: http://www.netlaughter.com/hillbilly.htm
Being you are a man of words thought you would like to add a few new meanings to your list. Love, C.

*** Special Free Offer! ***

Free 50 Minute Phone Card!
Click here: http://www.netlaughter.com/phonecard.htm

Free 50 Minute Phone Card!

*** FREE Catalog from Kennedy-Western University! ***

Earn your Bachelor's, Master's, or Doctorate degree at home or on the road (no classroom attendance required). Apply your work experience and previous education towards your degree. Study courses that relate directly to your profession and complete your degree in 12 to 18 months. Get your FREE catalogue now!

Click Here!

==
*** AWESOME FREEBIE! —> Find Old Friends! ***

"Looking for old high school friends on the Net?
Go to ClassMates.com!
Your 24-Hour Online High School Class Reunion.
Keep the promises you made at graduation to stay in touch.
ClassMates.com!!! Finding Old Friends!"

Click Here!
==

You received this email because someone visited our site and wanted to tell you about it. If you have questions, please see http://supertaf.com/faq.htm
The IP address of the person who sent you this email is: 64.12.101.177
If you never want to receive another email through our service, click here:
http://supertaf.com/optout.php?email=hglewis1@aol.com

Because the example in Figure 4-7 identifies the sender and specifies a prior relationship, the spam accusation would be difficult to implement (although I have no recollection of ordering a prior book by that author).

Figure 4-7. Avoiding the spam accusation.

Subj:	Save 30% on "Loyalty Rules! : How Today's Leaders Build Lasting Relationships" by Frederick F. Reichheld
Date:	8/25/ 1:12:37 AM Eastern Daylight Time
From:	book-news@amazon.com (Amazon.com)
To:	hglewis1@aol.com

Dear Herschell G. Lewis,

As someone who has purchased books by Frederick F. Reichheld in the past, you might like to know that "Loyalty Rules! : How Today's Leaders Build Lasting Relationships" is now available. You can order your copy at a savings of 30% by following the link below.

http://www.amazon.com/exec/obidos/ASIN/1578512050/ref=mk_pb_wzk

Amazon.com
It's trendy these days to decry a lack of loyalty among employers, employees, customers, and even investors, and blame it for everything from drops in business profitability to the decline of civilized society. But Frederick F. Reichheld, a Bain & Company director emeritus, insists that loyalty lives—and, in fact, remains a major reason for the success enjoyed by some of the leading names in both the Old and New Economies. Loyalty Rules, his follow-up to 1996's The Loyalty Effect, shows how...

To learn more about "Loyalty Rules! : How Today's Leaders Build Lasting Relationships," please visit the following page at Amazon.com:

http://www.amazon.com/exec/obidos/ASIN/1578512050/ref=mk_pb_wzk

Does a definitive definition of spam exist, one that can be applied universally without involving personal idiosyncrasies? Here are a few possibilities. And accept them as that—possibilities. Hundreds of others may exist.

First, purists insist that the recipient must opt into an e-mail list. That means an e-marketer should not gather a name under one circumstance or company name and then use that name for e-mail under another name.

Obviously, this interpretation would practically eliminate e-mail list rentals. Although it is admirable from a perfect world point of view, it is unworkable from a realistic point of view. The middle ground seems to be acknowledging the source when sending e-mail and using, initially at least, the same name and format through which the name was gathered.

So if an individual tendered his or her online address to subscribe to a newsletter, use the newsletter when contacting that person. Avoiding the accusation of spam is as easy as offering, in the newsletter, an opt-in link to whatever else you are selling or showing . . . and honoring the intention of the recipient who either says no or shows no reaction.

TIP

The shorter the message, the less likely it is that anyone will regard it as spam.

Shorter messages implicitly include less commercial pitch than longer messages. Figure 4-8 and Figure 4-10 exemplify the type of short message that has minimal irritation-factor because reading it takes so little time. Those who are interested will click on the link; however, those who aren't interested won't feel annoyed.

Figure 4-8. Less is more.

Subj:	**College Education Funding**
Date:	4/21 6:05:05 AM Pacific Daylight Time
From:	geoffrey_kasher@yahoo.com (Geoffrey Kasher)
To:	hglewis1@aol.com

Here is some information that you should find interesting.

(*continues*)

Figure 4-8. (*continued*)

This is not a download or an attachment, it is a direct link. Simply Click-Here to access the information.

Geoffrey Kasher
561-864-8316

Even if the message in Figure 4-8 arrived on the screen of some-one who had no prior relationship with the sender, it's unlikely to be regarded as spam because of its brevity. Short messages run less spam-risk than long messages.

When a recipient clicks on the link in Figure 4-8, the message in Figure 4-9 pops onto the screen. Many people will drop out at this point, sensing an electronic maze.

Figure 4-9. An electronic maze.

For Herschell

Providing *Valuable* Information
of Particular Interest to You
Compliments of
Geoffrey Kasher

You can see the advantage—and the disadvantage—of a one-sentence message in Figure 4-10. The advantage is a quick response, because the message is read quickly. The disadvantage is that the "sell" is simply a teaser, requiring a second step before see-ing actual information. (There is no excuse for the missing apos-trophe in "Don't," and the caps/lowercase technique betrays this e-mail as advertising.

Figure 4-10. Pros and cons of being brief.

Subj:	**RoadRage? Find em with their License plate# .... akephivox**
Date:	4/21 6:42:29 PM Pacific Daylight Time
From:	jajid@akephivox.ca
To:	bxtflx@aol.com

Incredible New Software Unlocks Secrets They Dont Want You To Know About

Click Here Now For Complete Details!

Should the e-mail in Figure 4-11 be considered spam, even though there aren't any specifics? To some people, the answer is yes; to others, it's no. A general rule seems to be that the more time an individual spends online, the more likely it is that an unsolicited message will be regarded as spam.

Always offering an opt-out is additional insurance against the spam-accusation. This is (in my opinion) mandatory when sending a first e-mail to someone who has not been expecting to hear from you.

Figure 4-11. Are you interested?

Subj:	**I thought u might be interested bky**
Date:	4/13 8:02:29 AM Pacific Daylight Time
From:	williamholistar1@altavista.com (William Holaster)
To:	gryphy@aol.com

Check out this link - I thought you might be interested in it - it's a RISK FREE, home business opportunity!

Find the best deals on the Web at AltaVista Shopping!
http://www.shopping.altavista.com

Understand, please: Offering an opt-out doesn't mean *suggesting* an opt-out. E-marketers with even a basic understanding of sales psychology can minimize opt-outs by wording them so the individual sees a sense of loss if he or she opts out.

Should e-marketers clean their lists once a year? Since e-mail is inexpensive, cleaning the list may be an expensive luxury that accomplishes only eliminating names that might respond later on. Of course, elimination of dead names is assumed.

Any e-marketer runs the automatic risk of spawning false spam complaints. That's part of doing business, just as for generations direct mail has generated hate mail. It's part of business, and running scared is no better an idea than running wild with the throttle wide open.

Spam or a Private/Public Service?

Ticketmaster.com once sent a series of e-mail messages about a forthcoming Bruce Springsteen concert. Was it regarded as spam? Hardly, and this is why not:

First, Ticketmaster e-mailed only people who already had bought tickets for the concert. What would the benefit of that be, since they already had their tickets? The e-mails were "helpful," describing ways to get to the venue. This sowed the field.

Then, after the concert, Ticketmaster.com sent more e-mails, this time with a link to a site where recipients could buy Springsteen CDs and memorabilia. The company reported a near-impossible 90 percent click-through rate, with a 25 percent sales conversion rate. Obviously, the preset attitude stemming from the first e-mail set a receptive attitude.

In the Eye of the Beholder

The purpose of this book isn't to serve as a primer on how to block spam. You wouldn't be reading this if you were solidly opposed to e-mail.

Thoughtful individuals recognize the wide disparity of messages that come their way online. One person's spam is another's salvation. And the person who raises a spam accusation against one message may respond positively to the next message in the queue.

The e-mail marketing community recognizes the need for opt-out as the proper solution *for individuals as individuals*. Attempting mass blockage denies message-acceptance rights to those who either do not object to whatever the communication might be or aggressively seek it out.

Logic seems to prevail in this section of an anti-spam online page:

What not *to do about spam*

There is one cardinal rule to remember when dealing with spammers and rogue sites: we must hold the high moral ground.

Therefore, when dealing with a spammer or a rogue site, don't:

- *Threaten violence or vandalism.*
- *Mailbomb the site.*
- *Mailbomb the alleged spammer, who may be an innocent third party such as myself.*
- *Ping-storm or SYN-flood the site.*
- *Hack into the site.*
- *Try in any way to bring the site down illegally.*

And above all else, don't use spam to fight spam.

This also applies in Usenet—don't follow up to spam postings, lest your posting also become spam.

A Peculiar Episode

The ultimate spam anecdote might be the actions of Californian Ellen Spertus, who in mid-2001 filed a lawsuit against a company called Kozmo.

When Spertus opted out of Kozmo, the company sent her an e-mail acknowledging the opt-out, naming new services in which she might be interested, and inviting her to opt back in. So she filed suit, accusing Kozmo of sending her spam.

The San Francisco Small Claims Division of the Superior Court of California agreed with her and awarded her $50 for the spam and $27.50 in court costs. Her claim was uncontested, but she probably will never collect because Kozmo, capitalized at $280 million (including $60 million from Amazon.com), closed its doors on almost the exact day Ellen Spertus won her judgment.

A Peculiar Conclusion

Jupiter Research estimates that there will be 268 billion e-mail messages in the year 2005, twenty-two times the number sent in the year 2000. That's considerably less than the IDC prediction of 35 billion per day. It also predicts there will be a four-tier procedure for e-mail delivery.

According to Jupiter, individuals would have primary and secondary in-boxes (paralleling first class and standard class mail categories). The top tier would be profiled delivery into the primary in-box, timed to fit the recipient's greatest receptivity. The second tier would reach the individual's primary in-box through enhanced fonts and images that, the research company said, would break through clutter. The third tier would be standard delivery to the primary in-box and the fourth tier would be bulk delivery to the secondary in-box.

Jupiter says this procedure would mean the end of spam. And, so it would, if implemented . . . until bulk e-marketers began infiltrating the primary boxes, and e-marketers to the third tier began attempting to gain greater attention by infiltrating the second tier in-boxes, and e-marketers found ways to disguise their nonprofiled messages as profiled messages.

"Please Read Our Privacy Policy"

A huge percentage of spam complaints stem from the individual's quick dismissal of one of two statements that often accompany a sign-up. The first: "Would you like to receive special offers from selected affiliate companies?" Two boxes exist; a dot is in the yes box, which means one needs a mouse movement and click to make a change. Leaving that box unchanged represents an opt-in, and resulting communications aren't spam.

The second statement is more direct, and we see it in sweepstakes and free offers: "By entering your online name you agree to receive notices of special promotions and discounts from our marketing partners." The wording may not be that straightforward, or it may be even more bald. The meaning is clear to those who read it: You're sacrificing privacy for opportunity.

The personal nature of e-mail masks—and in a sense betrays— the parallel to entering a sweepstakes by mail. Yes, sweepstakes are sweepstakes, online or in the mail. The difference, as is true of all comparisons between e-mail and snail mail, is one of perception. Those who get unsolicited sweepstakes offers in the mail may or may not know their names have been rented. The source is inconsequential, because all the recipient sees is another unsolicited offer in the mailbox. The e-mail psychology is infinitely more personal than that of direct mail. "Who are these people?" is an all too common reaction to an e-mail offer, even one that has a substantial attraction.

Name Harvesting

The popular auction site eBay Inc. has been a prime mover in lobbying Congress to pass a law preventing e-mail address harvesting.

Address harvesting—actually, name harvesting—refers to using powerful software programs to gather names, in bulk, from the Web. The software sweeps names from chatrooms, from commercial Web sites, and from any online source to which names are exposed.

The eBay argument is that the harvesters grab millions of names, which they use or sell to send illegal spam. One of eBay's lawyers stated that spammers have built substantial businesses by using software that automatically sucks in millions of e-mail addresses and spews them out again as spam.

So the old saw holds true: Spam is in the eye of the beholder. What leavens the mixture, and the conclusion is the presence or absence of *ethics*.

CHAPTER 5

That Magical Ingredient—Rapport

The impression of having an arm around the shoulder is the edge e-mail has over every other medium, whether mass communication, force-communication, or, yes, personal communication. (Actually, the impression of personal communication is the core of rapport.)

Generating genuine rapport requires more talent as a communicator than what has become a standard, almost computerized procedure—struggling to e-mail a tortured one-to-one message. The best targets are the most sophisticated, yet they also are the most likely to recognize and reject synthetic friendship.

Segmenting by What You Know

Reaching people within their individual experiential backgrounds is a major factor in establishing the type of rapport that translates into response.

One such marketing technique is the Cohorts approach (see Chapter 8), which identifies a number of discrete groups, making it possible to tailor the message so that it seems to cater to each group.

The examples of e-mail in Figure 5-1, Figure 5-2, Figure 5-3, and Figure 5-4 carry identical factual cores to four of the Cohorts demographic selections. Note the subtle differences in tone among Alec and Elyse, the affluent empty nesters in Figure 5-1; Jules and Roz, the affluent couple with kids in Figure 5-2; Maribeth, the educated working woman in Figure 5-3; and Stuart, the rich guy in Figure 5-4. A number of other segments were also developed for the e-mailing.

(This was an actual successful example. The company name and telephone number have been changed in the figures.)

(*text continues on page 92*)

Figure 5-1. Alec and Elyse.

Subject: **Alec, it occurs to me that you might want to do something nice. I can help.**

You and I don't need a special event to make a friend or a loved one feel special. In fact, I think you'll agree with me that nothing is more delightful than to receive a remembrance you weren't expecting . . . a remembrance for no reason at all except a spontaneous feeling of affection.

(I sent my sister, whom I haven't seen in almost a year, a dozen chrysanthemums. You can't imagine the pleasure it brought me when she called. She was literally in tears of happiness at my thoughtfulness. That doubled my own happiness.)

Now, this is the reason for my contacting you today: You're in a unique position with us. You're what we call a *Best Customer*. I can prove this to you very quickly:

Sunflowers has a special *private* Web site for our Best Customers. You have access to that private site. The general public doesn't. I invite you to send a dozen chrysanthemums to a loved one, right now. Of course, these are just one of a number of limited-quantity flowers, together with "sneak preview" opportunities, available only to you as a Best Customer. Many arrangements have a sophisticated "monochromatic" (one dominant color throughout) theme.

And you also should see the newest addition to the Sunflowers family: Our snow-white "BabyGap" Bouquet is codesigned by BabyGap.com and Sunflowers to create the *perfect* celebration of a new baby's arrival. What a remarkable value! The proud new parents get 20 pristine White Tulips with stems of pure white Waxflower . . . *plus* two pairs of white fleece socks, so baby's toes stay toasty warm . . . *plus* FREE shipping on Mom's next purchase from BabyGap.com. Click here for the BabyGap Bouquet: *[LINK]*

And click here to see all the other new and unusual arrangements we'll ship by FedEx overnight. *[LINK]*

Alec, I apologize if I've intruded today. But I really think this would be a wonderful day to surprise someone with a lovely gift of gorgeous superfresh flowers. I hope you agree. It's easy to be a hero.

With every good wish,
Jim Stern, for Sunflowers

To contact us, call 1-800 Sunflowers (1-800-555-5555). Customer Service is available 4:00 a.m. to 12:00 a.m. Pacific time, Monday to Friday, and 5:00 a.m. to 9:00 p.m., Saturday and Sunday.

Figure 5-2. Jules and Roz.

Subject: **Family happiness for you, Jules.**

Hi, Jules.

I'm contacting you personally because I have an idea to share with you. It may involve your spouse. Or, the two of you might want to team up on this.

(*continues*)

Figure 5-2. (*continued*)

Two factors brought this to mind. First, I see that you have elite status with us. You're one of a handful of individuals we call *Best Customers*.

Second, the day before yesterday, just because of a burst of love, I sent my wife a bouquet of graceful blue irises, from "Your loving family." I can't tell you what an emotional impact it made! Was it because it was a pure impulse "I love you" statement, not tied to any birthday or anniversary or holiday? I don't know. I only know that it's two days later and I'm still a champion and so are our kids.

So I'm writing to suggest you do the same.
Right now—today and tomorrow—we've set aside a special group of bouquets, *only* for our best customers. You can see them by clicking here: *[LINK]* This is a private page on our Web site. The general public will never see it. You can send flowers to your spouse. Or maybe the two of you or your family can send a "Just because we love you" bouquet to a loved one.

Because of our unique structure, we're able to give you a guarantee no local florist ever could: We *guarantee* that your bouquet will stay fresh for a full seven days. And better yet: Because we deliver by FedEx overnight, many of the blossoms will just be emerging into full bloom as they're delivered.

You also should see the newest addition to the Sunflowers family: Our snow-white "BabyGap" Bouquet is codesigned by BabyGap.com and Sunflowers to create the *perfect* celebration of a new baby's arrival. What a remarkable value! The proud new parents get 20 pristine White Tulips with stems of pure white Waxflower . . . *plus* two pairs of white fleece socks, so baby's toes stay toasty warm . . . *plus* FREE shipping on Mom's next purchase from BabyGap.com. Click here for the BabyGap Bouquet: *[LINK]*

How about it, Jules? Want to be a champion at home? It's simple. Just click here: *[LINK]*

It's a pleasure for me to share this happy thought with you.

Regards,
Jim Stern
Chairman, Sunflowers.com

To contact us, call 1-800 Sunflowers (1-800-555-5555). Customer Service is available 4:00 a.m. to 12:00 a.m. Pacific time, Monday to Friday, and 5:00 a.m. to 9:00 p.m., Saturday and Sunday.

Figure 5-3. Maribeth.

Subject: **Your private Web site, Maribeth, and how I used mine**

Maribeth, I suggest it may be time to "smell the roses."

I'll tell you why I'm contacting you today:

Just on a whim, I sent my Mom a bouquet of flowers. I didn't have a specific reason for sending the flowers. It's been a couple of months since we saw each other, and I suddenly realized she may have been as lonesome for me as I was for her. So, I sent her a bouquet.

She called me. She was crying—tears of happiness that her daughter had remembered her. "What makes these so wonderful," she said to me, "is that you didn't need a reason. It isn't my birthday and it isn't an anniversary and it isn't a holiday. That was the sweetest thing I can imagine."

So, I made my Mom happy. Now I think I'll send some flowers to my sister. She lives on the other coast, and we aren't as close as we should be. The flowers will help correct that.

How about you, Maribeth?

You're in an unusual position with us here at Sunflowers. We've chosen our list very carefully, and you're on our "Best Customers" roll. That means preferential treatment all the way.

(continues)

Figure 5-3. (*continued*)

For starters, we have some special bouquets. By "special," I mean they're available only to Best Customers because they're on a private Web page. You can get there by clicking here: *[LINK]*. The general public can't because they won't ever have that Web address.

Whether it's to your own mother, or to a relative, or to a business associate, the perfect time to send flowers is *when they aren't expecting it*. And as you know, you have two advantages when you order your flowers from Sunflowers: First, you know the flowers are fresh. In fact, they're guaranteed to stay fresh for at least seven days. (Try getting a guarantee like that from a local florist!) Second, because we ship by FedEx overnight, you know they'll be delivered with a flourish.

You also should see the newest addition to the Sunflowers family: Our snow-white "BabyGap" Bouquet is codesigned by BabyGap.com and Sunflowers to create the *perfect* celebration of a new baby's arrival. What a remarkable value! The proud new parents get 20 pristine White Tulips with stems of pure white Waxflower . . . *plus* two pairs of white fleece socks, so baby's toes stay toasty warm . . . *plus* FREE shipping on Mom's next purchase from BabyGap.com. Click here for the BabyGap Bouquet: *[LINK]*

Ordering couldn't be easier. Just click here: *[LINK]*

Oh, one more thought: How about *you*? Celebrate anything at all—even opening that bottle of Chateau Margaux you've been saving—by treating yourself to a bouquet. Every time you look at them, you'll be glad you're you.

Have a happy day!

Vickie Jones
Vice President, Sunflowers.com

To contact us, call 1-800 Sunflowers (1-800-555-5555). Customer Service is available 4:00 a.m. to 12:00 a.m. Pacific time, Monday to Friday, and 5:00 a.m. to 9:00 p.m., Saturday and Sunday.

Figure 5-4. Stuart.

> Subject: **Stuart, you're on this special preferred list.**

Hi, Stuart:

My friend, I'll tell you why I'm contacting you today.
If you're like I am, you'll be interested in the spectacular effect a little touch of love meant to my "significant other."

I sent her a bouquet of flowers. Well, okay, I had done that before . . . but always for a reason, her birthday or an anniversary or a holiday. This time I sent her an "I love you" bouquet *for no reason other than to tell her I love her*. Wow, what a reaction! You'd think I sent her a Jaguar convertible! She was in tears when she called to thank me.

So I'm contacting you to suggest that today might be the perfect day to send flowers to someone special—a friend, sis, your mother, a business colleague, anyone significant in your life. Why today? Because the most wonderful time for someone to get flowers is when she isn't expecting them.

And you share a major benefit. You're on our "Best Customers" list. That means you have access to the exclusive Best-Customers-Only Web site. That's where you'll find special arrangements and bouquets, including the latest monochromatic arrangements built around a single striking color—sort of like Regis Philbin's shirt and tie.
You know the benefit of having Sunflowers as your flower company. Every bloom is *guaranteed* fresh. (In fact, we guarantee they'll stay fresh for at least seven full days.) And because we ship by FedEx overnight, when you send a Sunflowers bouquet, you know you're making an elegant statement.

How about it, Stuart? Want to make somebody happy? Just click here: *[LINK]*

You also should see the newest addition to the Sunflowers family: Our snow-white "BabyGap" Bouquet is codesigned by BabyGap.com and Sunflowers to create the *perfect* celebration of a new baby's arrival. What a remarkable value!

(continues)

Figure 5-4. (*continued*)

The proud new parents get 20 pristine White Tulips with stems of pure white Waxflower . . . *plus* two pairs of white fleece socks, so baby's toes stay toasty warm . . . *plus* FREE shipping on Mom's next purchase from BabyGap.com. Click here for the BabyGap Bouquet: *[LINK]*

See how easy it is to make someone happy—including you? Why not click your way to mutual happiness right now!

For Sunflowers.com,
Jim Stern, Chairman

To contact us, call 1-800 Sunflowers (1-800-555-5555). Customer Service is available 4:00 a.m. to 12:00 a.m. Pacific time, Monday to Friday, and 5:00 a.m. to 9:00 p.m., Saturday and Sunday.

TIP

Make it both easy and profitable for recipients to respond. That means including the capability for your target individuals to separate automated responses from inquiries and comments. This not only helps reduce opt-outs but also maintains the image of customer control, a valuable component of virtual rapport.

As stated elsewhere in this text, rapport also depends on a conversational tone. Contractions are in: It's "I'll," not "I will" or the dreaded standoffish "I shall." And "I'll" is light years more rapport-laden than "We'll." Obviously, it isn't always possible to use first-person singular for a corporate commitment, but it is equally obvious that a *signed* e-mail should be from an individual.

What about second-person plurals? Does the phrase "those of you" kill response that might have come from a singular "only you"?

Not necessarily. This is where the e-marketer's knowledge of primitive psychology comes to the fore. Although suggesting that benefits are singular does help the one-to-one relationship, the assumption of a one-to-one relationship in an offer from a previously unknown source can have a *negative* effect when the recipient regards the message as an invasion of privacy.

Therefore, "You are one of the first to know about . . ." can be safer than "You are the first to know about . . ." And once again, the rule is not absolute because targets are not homogenous. This is an area worth major testing, especially for e-mails selling services rather than products.

Figure 5-5 is an example of useful information that is so self-centered and so without rapport that some people who might have responded to a warmer second-person approach probably bypassed the event. The pronoun "we" succeeds in establishing rapport only when it includes both parties so that the target doesn't feel left out.

Figure 5-5. Establishing rapport with pronouns.

Subj:	**Supply Chain Management - "Making the E-Leap",**
Date:	9:13:33 PM Pacific Daylight Time
From:	patty_smith@non.hp.com (SMITH,PATTY (Non-HP-Cupertino,ex1))
To:	HGLEWIS1@AOL.COM

Dear Herschell:
Hewlett-Packard Company has been walking-the-walk to incorporate the Internet in its business models. By focusing on processes, hp's business entities are able to transform themselves repetitively. Collaboration and trust are the operative words to gain flexibility and velocity for hp's supply chains. In this cooling and volatile economic environment, the pressure is up to lower inventory, reduce cycle times, and increase revenue and profit.

Visit www.supplychain.hp.com to explore the new world of business opportunity with Hewlett-Packard, and see how companies are finding profitable new ways to deliver value and capture market share.

(continues)

Figure 5-5. (*continued*)

"Making the E-Leap" Webcast

This webcast series is a good place to start, based on the ongoing exploration of Hewlett-Packard and its partners. It's an unprecedented chance to hear the stories of pioneers, firsthand. And our interactive capabilities give you and your customers the opportunity to ask questions of the experts.

The "Making the E-Leap" webcast series is a vehicle for sharing Hewlett-Packard's know-how, so that you and your customers can leverage the enormous opportunities posed by the Internet. In turn, we will pay close attention to the live participant interaction, collecting feedback to better serve you, your customers, and your partners.

Registration Information
Register now at www.supplychain.hp.com/webcasts

Upcoming LIVE webcasts:
- André Kuper, Hewlett-Packard, program manager and senior hp consultant on e-business transformation; "Pitfalls and opportunities of e-business transformation" April 12, 2001
- Lori Rhodig, Hewlett-Packard, R&D project manager, HP Design for Variety, "Design for Variety: enabling fast, flexible customization" April 24, 2001
- Anita Danford, HP Director, E-supply Chain Solutions; Greg Jacobus, HP Director, Procurement Risk Management; and Jeff McKibben, HP E-Procurement program manager, Enabling process transformation: critical success factors; May 10
All webcasts begin at 9:00 a.m. Pacific / 10:00 a.m. Mountain / 11:00 a.m. Central / 12:00 noon Eastern
Archived webcasts you might find interesting:
- Kevin Howard, Packaging Logistics Strategist, beyond postponement: regional logistics effectiveness
- Sam Szteinbaum, Business Manager, sustaining profitability: achieving growth as a market leader
- Gilles Bouchard, Vice President, virtual collaboration: winning in the volatile pc market

- Alastair Atkinson, Senior Managing Consultant, outsourcing manufacturing-creating a value collaboration network
- Dave Blanchar and Jim Anderson, total customer solutions: flexible platforms for telecom and beyond
- Corey Billington, Vice President, Supply Chain Services
- Petere Miner, bringing the e into logistics
- Sam Mancuso and Uli van der Meer, value collaboration networks: hp's solution vision
- Swagata Saha, collaborative design: gaining flexibility and speed
- Greg Daggett, channel collaboration: hp's automatic inventory replenishment program

Bob Thought You Might Like This

The assumption of a relationship is a sort of pseudorapport mechanism. Is it ethical? No. Is it effective? Yes or no, depending on the sophistication of the recipient. (There are two examples in Chapter 4: "John thought you might like this" and "Sue thought you might like this."

Figure 5-6 is an e-mail from "Bob." It's another example of this technique, borrowed from a venerable—and, one would think, worn-out—direct-mail ploy. The intention, obviously, is to ride on the coattails of preestablished rapport with someone whose name is known to the recipient. Everybody knows someone named Bob. The problem with this gimmick is that it has become so commonplace that it is now has become (to the best prospects) instantly recognizable as what it is—a gimmick.

Figure 5-6. Bob thought you might like this.

Subj:	**Bob thought you might like this**
Date:	4/30 1:37:40 AM Pacific Daylight Time
From:	willard2722gey@gte.com (willard2722gey@gte.com)
To:	3783@aol.com (3783@aol.com)

(continues)

Figure 5-6. (*continued*)

Give your family great program choices and save money!

Get up to 125 Channels of Cable/Digital TV with
NO monthly fees!
Quality family channels like Disney, History, Discovery, Cartoon Network, Lifetime, and A&E.

Movie channels like HBO, Showtime, Starz, Cinemax and more.

Sports stations like ESPN, ESPN2 and many more.

Save on your cable/satellite now

Figure 5-7 is of the same genre. The personal references in this *unsigned* communication—"I've been really busy with the kids and soccer practice this season. What's going on with you?"—are meant to suggest a personal relationship.

Figure 5-7. More news from Bob.

Subj:	**I think it is time we talked**
Date:	7/2 11:59:54 PM Pacific Daylight Time
From:	ewa1061759@msn.com (ewa1061759@msn.com)
To:	3087@yahoo.com (3087@yahoo.com)

Hey,

Got your message a few days ago but I've been really busy with the kids and soccer practice this season. What's going on with you? I meant to tell you I was working with a group that was able to take my credit card bills and cut them in half! And no, its not some sort of BS home loan or anything.

It's a pretty cool deal, if your interested the site is:

http://www.freehostplanet.com/~freeuser987/sanfrancisco/

I hope I did the link right. Let's get together for a beer next week after work.

Later

Bob and his troops represent a dangerous trend, one that can damage e-mails actually stemming from an existing relationship.

The Perils of Production

Visualize a letter from your Aunt Tillie. You might have one of the following reactions:

- Your reaction is *A*—The envelope has her address in the upper left corner and yours in the center.

- Your reaction is *B*—Here comes a letter from someone who wants to establish the same rapport you have with your Aunt Tillie. The envelope has a "Wow, are you going to be surprised!" legend.

- Your reaction is *C*—And yet another envelope from a sender who thinks, "Aunt Tillie had better be brought into the twenty-first century if she wants her letters to be read." The envelope is a custom-converted photograph of people surfboarding in Hawaii, with handwriting or typing over the photograph.

Reaction *A* is familial. You're comfortable but unexcited. Rapport is a given, a preexisting open gate into the comfort zone. Suspicion, doubts, and wariness are suppressed by family receptivity.

So what is missing? It's the excitement and anticipation stemming from newness and novelty.

Reaction *B* is skepticial, but leaving a hole for optimism. As a typical twenty-first century consumer or businessperson, you've heard that song before. Yeah, sure, I'll be surprised. I'll be surprised if I'm surprised. But maybe this message actually will be a happy surprise.

So what is missing? Trust. You're expecting trouble, because you're looking at a loose, unspecific promise of a type that has been broken before, maybe many times.

Reaction *C* is the reaction to any advertising message you regard as competently prepared. You accept it for what it is—an advertising message. You know someone has produced this message and you aren't the only one to get it.

So what is missing? It's the feeling of individuality or exclusivity, the feeling that the sender actually sought out—from all the potentials—you.

You can see the positives and negatives of each reaction. You can see, too, that any message able to combine the rapport-enhancing artlessness of the letter from Aunt Tillie, the excitement potential of "Wow!" and the professionalism of a well-produced advertising message may bring ultimate power to the communication, the combination of rapport, excitement, and professionalism—a rare and unbeatable combination that opens the psychographic lock.

Now you open the envelope. What do you see?

If you see a handwritten note, your reaction is *A*. If you see a typewritten note, your reaction is *B*. And if you see a bunch of cartoons, your reaction is *C*.

Here, reaction *A* maintains the rapport-pace. That's good. You react, too, to the lack of variety and reader fatigue if the note runs more than a few paragraphs. That is bad.

Reaction *B* is business comfort, also good. You react, too, to the immediate recognition that this *is* less personal than a handwritten note, so rapport can be neither immediate nor as profound. That's bad.

Reaction *C* is your reaction to novelty, an interest-grabber. That's good. You react, too, to the quick realization that the novelty is a gimmick, an artifice unrelated to you, specifically. That's bad.

The point of this mini-exercise: Which envelope treatment and which letter will be most likely to generate rapport?

Aunt Tillie faces a so-what reaction. That is a problem. Another problem (squared, because it isn't Aunt Tillie) attends both commercial-looking and overproduced e-mail. Rapport becomes secondary to production.

TIP

If you think *any* e-mail has a problem establishing or maintaining rapport, you understand the purpose of this book. The volume, intensity, and irritation potential of the medium warrant a thoughtful "How do I couch this?" preanalysis.

Now, please, please don't interpret negative analyses of nontext as an attack on produced e-mail. Rather, it's an attack on e-mail that substitutes the ink in the pen for the words flowing out of that pen. The sender thinks he or she is engendering rapport but doesn't know what the elements are. Pronouncements, however gussied up and accompanied by laser light shows, are outside the arena of rapport. They can fail not because they use the wrong tool but because they use too many tools.

The Maintenance Factor

Maintaining rapport isn't as difficult as establishing rapport. We know that from individual interpersonal relationships.

Establishing rapport means overcoming an obstacle—whether that obstacle is suspicion, boredom, lack of interest, prior bonding with a competitor, or assumption of nonrelevance. Maintaining rapport means fending off fungal encroachments by any of those factors.

A simple and prime key is the word *benefit*, which, when accompanied by apparent sincerity, adds a continuing stream of cement to the bond between e-mail marketer and e-mail responder. As other chapters of this book explore, constant contact may or may not represent benefit. Newsletters, free or discount offers, and "private club" propositions have the potential for maintaining rapport, but they cannot assure it.

Maintaining rapport is obviously a creative challenge. That challenge is not to be taken lightly, considering the increasing difficulty of reaching a rapport plateau as e-mail marketing reaches competitive saturation.

TIP

An underused tool is an occasional thank you or "Just want to tell you how much we appreciate your being a member of our family" note from the top executive, with no commercial overtone.

Figure 5-8 is an example of one company's strategy for maintaining rapport. What is the purpose of this e-mail? No commercial offer is included, so the purpose is to establish rapport by primitive stroking. The concept is sound, although the message becomes wordy and self-serving—and might have had a greater rapport-building effect had it ended more quickly.

Figure 5-8. Thank you for shopping at NetGrocer.

Subj:	**Thank you for shopping at NetGrocer**
	5:42:41 PM Pacific Daylight Time
From:	ervice@NetGrocer.com
To:	hglewis1@aol.com

Dear "hglewis1",

We wanted to personally welcome you to the NetGrocer family, we're thrilled to have you aboard. By selecting to sign up at NetGrocer you have shown yourself to be progressive and enlightened, just the kind of people that make our family great. Now it's our turn to earn and keep your business every day. We believe that by providing extraordinary service and value— with our low prices, nationwide delivery coverage and our easy product sorting and selection features—you'll appreciate the difference in shopping smarter and faster.

We like having you around and encourage you to visit NetGrocer often. We will be expanding our product selection, and we will regularly feature outstanding special values that represent the best deals in grocery shopping.

Just look at a sampling of what we can do for those looking to make their shopping easier and help plan their meals better...

Check out our sorting features— wherever you see products displayed, sort them based on cost-per-unit or any of several nutritional factors. Just try that in your local supermarket, but be sure to bring plenty of help because you'll be there awhile!.

How about our shopping lists and recurring orders— imagine how convenient you'll find having a similar order delivered to your home or office on a regular basis. If we made it any easier, we'd have to select the products for you!

And it doesn't stop there, more information on the above features and lots more is available from the help link of our home page.
Last but not least, please remember that NetGrocer is YOUR service... we made it for you! We welcome your input and actually respond. If you have any comments about NetGrocer's site, suggestions as to how we can improve our service, or even if you're just feeling lonely, simply drop us a line at service@netgrocer.com. After all, you're part of the family now!

Sincerely,

The NetGrocer Team

Dire Warnings

Can you generate rapport with a dire warning? Certainly. Again, visualize a close friend who cares about your health or your appearance or your finances. That person wouldn't mince words, wouldn't carefully couch his or her rhetoric, wouldn't worry about offending you because the comment is obviously sincere. So here is another creative challenge: mirroring that friendly concern.

Which of these subject lines better mirrors a dire warning that establishes or maintains rapport?

- You don't have to grow old.

- Do you want to die too soon?

Analyze them. The first is a statement most people have heard many times in advertising. It's both safe and clear. The second is a challenge, almost close to an insult. In fact, some may regard it as intrusive, which parallels an insult.

Does that mean the second approach is too dangerous to be effective e-mail? On the contrary, it can succeed because the potential for rapport outweighs the potential for insult. Yes, some people will turn away. But grabbing and shaking attention with apparent sincerity is e-mail weaponry, designed and crafted to overcome automatic rejection.

The second sentence, then, has greater rapport potential.

Here are additional examples:

- Save 20 percent on anything you buy this week.

- Why spend more money than you have to?

Again, the first sentence is a straightforward and recognizable promotional statement. The second is a challenge, worded the way a friend might comment. The second has greater rapport potential.

Building a Rapport Test

This isn't nuclear science, nor is it absolute. People don't run on tracks, and testing always is in order. To construct a rapport test, first create a standard sales message that parallels strong, dynamic advertising.

Then create a second message paralleling what you would say—verbally—to a friend when you're genuinely interested in helping that friend's health or fortune. If you split the messages among your target groups, you'll have a quick answer.

Psychology Over Technology: A Valid Conclusion?

Two venerable rules of force-communication may or may not apply to this new medium, which breaks so many rules:

- *Rule 1*: Relevance outsells heavy production.

- *Rule 2*: Relevance outsells personalization.

The computer made it possible for a communication to be both relevant and personalized. Laser-personalized letters have been common since the 1980s.

One reason so much mud is swirling around in the waters is that suppliers—from Webmasters to software producers to consultants to researchers to technical message manufacturing companies—often report and quote opinions or self-serving advertising as though those opinions or advertising were fact-based.

The problem is compounded because in a field as gigantic and diverse as e-mail, invariably a direct marketer can find results justifying a claim. That the claim represents a lower percentage of overall success than an opposing claim is inconsequential to the claimer. The e-marketer believes that if the procedure works for this project at this particular time, it is sufficient . . . and enough to justify full-page advertisements in the trade magazines, exhibits at trade shows, and a flood of direct mail and telephone calls.

The overriding consideration has to be that nothing is absolute, and the individual e-marketer has the best gauge at the fingertips—a test of one approach against another.

But a growing mountain of evidence supports e-mail on the generic level. In 2001, a company called InPhonic tested e-mail against banners to 10 million consumers. The company reported that switching from banner ad campaigns to direct e-mail resulted in a click-through rate increase from 0.5 percent to nearly 4 percent.

A (Dangerous) General Rule

I venture, here in print, an opinion based on both personal experience and results reported by sources I regard as relatively statesmanlike.

The nineteenth-century French writer Alexandre Dumas was 150 percent correct when he jibed, "All generalizations are false, including this one." But we have to start somewhere.

So, this next tip is the start:

Text tends to outpull HTML when your message suggests urgency. HTML tends to outpull text when your message suggests artistry.

You say that tip is simplistic? Obvious? Full of holes and exceptions? Certainly. But add one more adjective: logical.

Instead of e-mail, visualize its closest parallel, head-to-head speech. If your message is urgent, embellishments damage it by diluting the urgency. A drowning man doesn't have time to create a sign or to compose a poetic message. He screams an unvarnished, "Help!"

Similarly and contrarily, whipping up an emotional reaction to a relatively tranquil message is far more difficult with words alone than with both words and images.

TIP

The more technically oriented your targets are, the more likely it is that they will prefer text to HTML. That seems wrong at face value, but many who have tested both types or sent both simultaneously seem to feel HTML works best with those who aren't technically adept. Test it.

Two mid-2001 tests are worthy of exploration. Northwest Airlines reported sending messages with Flash animation and sound and a similar text-only message to groups of about 50,000 each of its WorldPerks members who had opted in to receive promotional e-mail. According to the airline, the click-through rate for the Flash animation version was 18 percent; for the text version, 6 percent.

A company called ETunnels sent e-mail to 45,000 business-to-business customers—one-third text, one-third standard HTML, and one-third complex HTML resembling a multimedia brochure. ETunnels said the text version achieved a 0.1 percent click-through rate, standard HTML a 1.4 percent click-through rate, and the complex HTML a 2.1 percent click-through rate.

In analyzing what appears to be a clear victory for the more heavily produced versions, two things remain: (1) the message content, which gives strength to text, may or may not have adhered to the "urgency" principle; and (2) the unreported response rate, which—as many sites featuring entertainment as a visitor-attraction device will testify—can have little relationship with the click-through rate.

As e-mail matures, the ratio of those who have the capability of receiving Flash and other sophisticated technologies increases. Catering to the technology may produce artificial response. So, the value of testing, not only for click-throughs but also for identifiable response, is ongoing. (See Chapter 16.)

In between urgency and artistry are many messages that do not qualify for either classification. For these, testing can bring conclusions that are far more useful than any prefabricated opinions.

And prefabricated opinions abound! A communicator who has no familiarity with HTML or its increasingly popular expansion, rich media, is hardly likely to endorse these methods. A company that has spent hundreds of thousands of dollars advertising its rich media capability is hardly likely to suggest simple text to a client.

Don't succumb to the temptation to use all the gimmicks just because you or someone in your office knows how to construct them. If you use HTML for its valuable embedded linking capability, that makes more sense than using HTML because you know how. The assumption that the medium is the message has damaged many e-mail campaigns.

The Above-the-Fold Semirule

Disclosing the most pertinent information "above the fold"—that is, before the reader has to scroll downward—has become a popular rule for e-marketers who believe that keeping the entire promotion within the smallest possible window is a solid sales technique.

But is it?

In most cases, it probably is. But the reason for any hedging is the difference between targets and prior interest or information. Attitude "A": Forcing the reader to scroll down can result in an annoyed click out of the e-mail. Attitude "B": Spilling out the gist too quickly is poor sales technique.

The best use of this semirule is to have it handy and decide whether or not to implement it on a case-by-case basis.

E-Marketers Tout What They Use

In a 2001 report, Jupiter Communications stated that rich media e-mails were delivering higher response rates—10 percent to 40 percent—than plain text or HTML messages.

(Other research had indicated an ongoing drop in typical e-mails, from about 18 percent in 2000 to 5 percent to 10 percent by mid-2001.)

An e-mail vendor was quoted in a trade publication as saying her two biggest clients "prefer to send image-embedded messages." The validity of this statement was called into question because her company specializes in image-embedded messages.

So many analyses are out of sync with one another that the individual e-marketer can't predraw a conclusion. Is rich media response large enough to support the additional cost of rich media? Does your message pull better in rich media than HTML? Better in HTML than in plain text? Then test. That's the best advice for what need not be a dilemma: Test. (If you don't have the money to pay for produced messages or the capability of producing HTML, the answer is staring you in the face: Go with text or don't use e-mail at all.)

Most packaged e-mail software includes automatic sensors that detect the recipient computer's capability of receiving HTML. The message goes out as text to computers that can't read HTML and as HTML to those that can. For example, a company named FloNetwork has a "sensing technology" that tells the sender whether to transmit rich text, HTML, or plain text—a valuable capability because some users report computer lockups caused by messages their computers couldn't decode.

The proliferation of new technologies may soon make the capability problem obsolete. But what doesn't become obsolete is the ongoing argument over whether the medium's capability is a factor in establishing the effectiveness of the message. History goes both ways: Dependence on technical effects does little to enhance the success of a television commercial; but the develop-

ment of morphing technology has changed forever the illus-
trative potentials of both television and motion pictures.

TIP

E-mail isn't a Web site. Loading an e-mail message with photos and graphics can
be counterproductive if the e-mail seems to be a mini-Web site. Many e-marketers
report better results from e-mail that builds a desire to "click here," taking the individual to the Web site.

Get to the Point

One of the Great Laws of force-communications: Get to the point.
This Law is squared . . . no, cubed . . . in e-mail. The typical online
visitor always looks in his or her mailbox first, when signing on to the
Internet; but the amount of time is finite, regardless of the number
of messages. Media merchant bank and private equity investor Vero-
nis Suhler says its research indicates an average total of only twenty
minutes a day online, regardless of the number of messages or other
Internet use. The accuracy of that number may be in question, but
the need for specifics isn't.

The combination of bullet-like terseness and friendliness is a
creative challenge. Meeting the challenge will result in increased
response and fewer opt-outs—and that combination is the best way
to keep score.

Newsletters that collapse into commercialism spawn opt-outs
because they don't make a point; they become mere carriers of business offers.

Take a look at Figure 6-1 and Figure 6-2. Figure 6-1 is an e-mail
newsletter that emphasizes its commercial content so thoroughly it
never gets to the point. Figure 6-2 promotes a free conference, but
instead of making a quick point, it seems to take forever to suggest a
benefit that comes from attending the conference.

(*text continues on page 118*)

Figure 6-1. Get to point.

Subj:	Get on the fast track to savings, Herschell, with your Travel Newsletter!
Date:	6:09:09 PM Pacific Daylight Time
From:	info@coolsavings.com (CoolSavings)
Sender:	info@coolsavings.com
Reply-to:	info@coolsavings.com (CoolSavings)
To:	hglewis1@AOL.COM

```
************************************************************
                    Travel Newsletter
************************************************************
```

Hi Herschell,

All aboard! This month's newsletter has plenty of stops, including train travel tips and scenic savings.

_____

Brought to you by Overstock.com

_____

Get $10 off your 1st purchase of $50 on great travel merchandise and more at Overstock! Plus, Overstock now offers great savings on hotel and travel reservations from all over the world! Up to 65% off—check it out today! Click Here

_____

Cool Info

_____

Rail is Real
Introduce your family to train travel! They'll enjoy the

(continues)

Figure 6-1. (*continued*)

scenery, you'll enjoy the savings and getting there can be
part of your vacation.
Click Here

This Cool Info is brought to you by OneTravel.com.
Click Here

Featured this Month

Whether you're planning a summer vacation or spring day
outing, eBags has what you need to get packing. Visit today
to save!
Click Here

Save up to 80% off original catalog prices on first-quality
Lands' End overstock merchandise!
Click Here

Herschell's Squeals of the Day

Hotwire
* Save up to 40% on airfare, hotel rooms and rental cars,
  even at the last minute! SAVE at Hotwire today!
  Click Here

Orvis.com
* Get 35% off women's Microfiber Travel Pant Sets at Orvis!
  Click Here

Entertainment.com
* Save up to 50% on restaurants, hotels, airfare and
  attractions on your vacation! Get $5 off the
  Entertainment Book today!
  Click Here

OneTravel.com
* Sample Southern hospitality starting at $114 roundtrip
  from OneTravel.com!
  Click Here

Vacationbook.com
* Vacation in your choice of destinations for 4 days & 3
  nights for only $129! Book TODAY and receive a bonus trip
  to Puerto Vallarta, Mexico for FREE!
  Click Here

Barnes & Noble.com
* Explore hundreds of travel books and save up to 20%!
  Click Here

Half.com
* Get DVDs, CDs and video games up to 90% off at Half.com.
  Plus, new customers get $5 off a $10 purchase!
  Click Here

Olive Garden
* Treat yourself to a fun night of great Italian cuisine
  with a FREE $25 gift certificate for The Olive Garden!
  Click Here

_____

My 2 Cents

_____

(continues)

Figure 6-1. (*continued*)

Check back next month!

Discounts from over 4,000 Restaurants!

Get 10% cash back on meals at participating restaurants.
Click below:
Click Here

Herschell, did you know?

The number of Amtrak passengers that travel in the New
York-Washington corridor is enough to fill 121 airline
flights per day.

Source: Amtrak.com

"Tell A Friend & Win" Sweepstakes

Ain't it GRAND? You and one of your friends could split
$$$ ONE GRAND $$$ in our "Tell A Friend & Win" Sweepstakes!
Click now to enter this month's sweepstakes.
Click Here

Click below for more Travel savings:
Click Here

Click below to update your member profile:
Click Here

You received this e-mail because you requested that
newsletters be sent to you at "hglewis1@aol.com".
If you feel that you have received this message in error,
or if you no longer wish to receive our Travel
Newsletter, please click below:
Click Here

Thank you for reading the CoolSavings Travel
Newsletter :-)

Figure 6-2. Where is benefit?

Subject:	U.S.S.B.A. online event!
Date:	1:48:52 PM Pacific Daylight Time
From:	J01553@intramaildirect.com (Great Plains Software)
Reply-to:	J01553@intramaildirect.com
To:	HGLEWIS1@AOL.COM

****
This mail is never sent unsolicited. This is an internet.com
mailing! You have subscribed to receive this information at
NewMedia / internet.com.
To unsubscribe please click on the link below:
http://www.intramaildirect.com/opt.asp?mc=161747433339&j=J01553
Review your subscriptions!
http://www.intramaildirect.com/01235/update.htm
****
It takes a lot more than a web site to build your business on the Internet.

If you want to create a truly effective online presence and grab your fair share of
the giant e-commerce pie, you need a strategy and an action plan. That's why I
urge you to accept this important invitation . . .

(continues)

Figure 6-2. (*continued*)

In May, the U.S. Small Business Administration and Great Plains, with the help of Compaq Computer Corporation are conducting a FREE online conference especially for growing businesses like yours. If you would like to know how to get started in e-commerce the RIGHT way, this unique online conference is for you!

IMPORTANT: All you need to join the online conference is access to the web and a telephone. There is NO special software needed and NOTHING to download.

"How to Put the Internet to Work in Your Business"
A FREE sixty-minute online conference — for growing businesses

Guest Speaker
Senior Consultant, Steven S. Little from Inc. Business Resources

Held live on two dates — your choice:

*** Wednesday, May 9   11:00 am EDT
*** Wednesday, May 16   2:00 pm EDT

Register Now At:
http://ecommerce.regsvc.com/index.asp?site=21
Or call toll free: 800-801-9473

At each event, we'll hold a drawing for a
FREE Compaq iPAQ Personal Audio Player.
When you register and attend, you could win!

Hosted by:
The U.S. Small Business Administration and Great Plains, with the help of Compaq Computer Corporation, will provide expert advice on your e-business strategies.

Why are we making "How to Put the Internet to Work in Your Business" available to you online, absolutely free? Our mission is to show forward-looking executives

at growing businesses new ways to seize e-commerce opportunities.
When you attend this information-packed online conference, you'll learn:

* How the SBA can go to work for you NOW—and at no cost. (It's worth attending our online seminar for this information alone!)
* How to choose a winning e-commerce strategy—options and opportunities
* How to increase the lifetime value of your customers
* How to use inbound and outbound e-mail to find and keep customers
* Proven ways to drive traffic to your web site
* The value of an integrated and flexible software and hardware solution
* How the right solution can grow with you and keep pace with your changing business needs

You will also see real-time demonstrations of the latest accounting and business management software.

If you're looking for new and effective ways to unlock the profit-potential of the Internet, "How to Put the Internet to Work in Your Business" is for you!

Register right now for the date most convenient to you. (No Obligation of course) After you register, we will email you the private conference web site address and toll free conference number to listen to the presentation.

Register at http://ecommerce.regsvc.com, or call toll free: 800-801-9473.

I know you will find this important online event of tremendous value. That's a personal promise.

Sincerely,

Karen Edwards
Great Plains

The support given by the U.S. Small Business Administration to this activity does not constitute an express or implied endorsement of any cosponsors or participant's options, products, or services. All SBA programs or cosponsored programs are extended to the public on a non-discriminatory basis.
SBA Auth No. 00-7630-37.

Little Words Mean a Lot

The word *free* is one of the most abused of all e-mail adjectives. Quite logically, marketers use the word to attract the eye; and equally logically, no astute marketer gives away something for nothing.

So, almost invariably, the word *free* has a hook. Figure 6-3 is an example of a free offer that depends on a $39.95 shipping and handling charge and a purchase commitment only revealed deep in the text.

Figure 6-3. Is it really free?

Subject:	Get a FREE DIRECTV Satellite TV System!
Date:	11:07:04 PM Pacific Daylight Time
From:	traffix@response.etracks.com (Traffix)
To:	hglewis1@aol.com

ATTENTION: hglewis1@aol.com,
You have been selected to receive a FREE* DIRECTV Satellite Entertainment System with FREE* standard professional installation! You pay only a $39.95 shipping and handling charge - saving you more than $250!
Click here!
This strictly limited-time offer will enable you to enjoy hundreds of channels of movies, sports, pay-per-view and more—TV as it's meant to be, with digital quality audio and video!
There is no mistake. Your FREE DIRECTV Satellite Entertainment System with FREE standard professional installation is waiting for you - but you must respond soon.
If I do not hear from you within 7 days this offer will go to someone else. Please do not allow that to happen!
Click here!
Stacie Miller

Authorization Manager

Satellite Concepts
P.S. This may be your final notice regarding the FREE DIRECTV Satellite Entertainment System.

*For free satellite system: Subscriber must install the satellite system within 30 days of receipt of equipment, or be subject to a one-time penalty of $125 (barring any delays that are the responsibility of Satellite Concepts and its installers). For installation offer: Limited time offer for new residential customers only who purchase a DIRECTV system, schedule an installation by 06/17, and activate DIRECTV programming ($21.99 a month) or above by 07/14. This offer is for one free standard installation per household. Installation of additional receivers and custom installation available for a charge. Programming, pricing, terms and conditions subject to change. Hardware and programming sold separately. Pricing is residential. Tax is not included. DIRECTV, Inc. and the cyclone design logo are trademarks of DIRECTV, Inc., a unit of Hughes Electronics Corp. Offer may not be valid in all areas.
Shipping and Handling fee is $39.95 and is not refundable.
This offer is brought to you by Traffix. If you do not wish to receive future promotions from Traffix, click here to unsubscribe.

Figure 6-3 shows how this old telemarketing ploy has adapted to e-mail. The word free is conditional, as opposed to actually free. Can one get the satellite dish without subscribing? No. Note the aster-isked wording: "Subscriber must install the satellite system within 30 days of receipt of equipment, or be subject to a one-time penalty of $125 (barring any delays that are the responsibility of Satellite Con-cepts and its installers). For installation offer: Limited time offer for new residential customers only who purchase a DIRECTV system, schedule an installation by 06/17, and activate DIRECTV program-ming ($21.99 a month) or above by 07/14."

Despite misuse by marketers, the word *free* still is a turn-on word. Individual words can turn on or turn off a targeted individual. For example, the message in Figure 6-4 exemplifies why trigger words such as *important* have lost much of their psychological impact. The value of a database in structuring the message can bring specificity to terminology.

For example, the word *sex* is usually an acceptable word in the subject line to people under age 35. However, it may be an uncomfortable word to those over age 50 and would probably cause a quick click-away in those over age 65. So the e-marketer might use the dynamic word for the younger group and substitute the word *love* or even use a different approach for older groups.

More obvious are expressions such as "cool" and "y'all" and "Hi, there," each of which can build or diminish rapport. The primitive psychologist in each of us as communicators can come to the fore when we know more about the demographic/psychographic profile of our targets.

Figure 6-4. Trigger words loose their impact.

Subject:	Important notice . 1025801
Date:	8/30/ 12:00:37 AM Eastern Daylight Time
From:	an1mkoatley@msn.com (an1mkoatley@msn.com)
To:	7786@gte.com (7786@gte.com)
CC:	[I've eliminated a long list of online names]

Vegas ON-NET
Play real casino games online play for real cash or for fun!
-BlackJack
-Slots
-Pai-gow
-3 poker games
-Roulette
-Bingo
-Jacks or Better
-Baccarat
-10% Bonus of first deposit
-We are giving away Huge prizes click the link below to view them!
Click Here

The Psychology of Punctuation

Credibility is the key to persuasion. And it actually can happen that punctuation is a key to credibility.

The benefit of knowing the rules of punctuation's impact is that the rules are so, so easy to apply. For example:

- A question mark is automatically interactive, signaling implicit reader involvement.

- Two exclamation points are weaker than one, because they betray the false excitement behind them. A single exclamation point is sufficient exclamation and has the capability of verisimilitude, which doubled exclamation points do not.

- A colon is a psychological forcer, pushing the reader into what follows because it projects the concept of incompleteness of what has been said so far.

- An asterisk suggests that the statement to which it is attached may not be entirely true. Use asterisks with caution because people are geared to anticipate seeing evidence of an exception. Another negative aspect of asterisks: Looking for the corresponding asterisk at the end of the message breaks up the flow and impact of the text. (Notice the use of a colon in the previous construction.)

- Among a comma's many uses is separation of elements in a series. For clarity, don't skip the comma between the penultimate and the final items in a series—for clarity, it would be "chicken, beans, and rice," not "chicken, beans and rice."

- A dash has more force than an ellipsis (ellipsis = three dots).

In extended text, punctuation plays a useful role; in the "punchy" text that so much e-mail represents, punctuation plays a vital role.

The Pros and Cons of Rich Media

A great deal of information about the differentials between text, HTML, and rich media is covered in Chapter 16, so why duplicate it here? Because what is covered in this chapter isn't duplication. Here we're discussing sales psychology, rather than technology.

Rich media are well-named. They include the color, graphics, great fonts, and other appurtenances one associates with HTML— plus audio and/or video, including "streaming" pictures with sound.

The standard arguments against rich media parallel the standard arguments old-timers heard against television in the 1950s:

- Not everybody can receive them.

- They add great expense to any message.

- You can't enjoy the quick turnaround implicit in straight text messages.

The arguments are true, of course. In the twenty-first century, although television is almost universal, not everyone has cable or a satellite dish. Production is infinitely more expensive than radio. And the concept of going live with a television commercial turns even the hardiest veteran an unpleasant shade of green.

TIP

If you want your HTML or rich media e-mail message to reach everybody, don't assume universal HTML compatibility or knowledge. Prepare the message in a text version as well.

The Edge Over Direct Mail

When an marketer mails an offer, the only information that comes back is either a hard response or a "nixie" (undeliverable mail).

> When a marketer e-mails an offer, a huge benefit opens up, one taken advantage of by too few e-marketers. The e-marketer can determine not only who has responded but also who has opened the e-mail and not responded.

TIP

When you have sent several e-mail offers a recipient has opened but not acted on, test one of these:

- A more dynamic, more aggressive approach

- A discount strongly tied to an expiration date

- A more personalized, one-to-one message that uses guilt or exclusivity as the motivator

- A change of format, to or from HTML or rich media

One Noteworthy Test

A test by Kawasaki Motors Corp. in 2001 sent rich media (audio- and video-enabled) e-mail to 30,000 consumers, primarily lists bought from publications or organizations associated with auto racing. Half the recipients were sent the promotion of a good times sweepstakes; half were sent information about a good times giveaway.

The sweepstakes featured a new Chevrolet Silverado. The giveaway featured either $500 in free accessories or no money down on a Kawasaki Vulcan Cruiser.

Kawasaki reported that response to the sweepstakes was 28 percent, while response to the giveaway was 19 percent.

Huge numbers! But does the result indicate that sweepstakes are better response generators than giveaways?

Not at all. If the purpose was to test the two techniques against each other, the rewards should have been parallel. Responders to the sweepstakes represent bulk greed-driven entries. Responders to the giveaway obviously were more Kawasaki-oriented. So, in the absence of follow-up reports, we might conclude that lower front-end results might mean a more profitable end-result for the company.

Attention Spans Are Fragile

Yes, the tighter your relationship with an individual, the longer your e-mail message can be. But take no one for granted. Remember where you are—on the Web, where even your most dedicated advocate has a finger planted on the mouse.

No matter what the relationship is, you have to grab a person's attention. You have to make a clear, compelling, and quick statement. And you have to remember your competition—not only other commercial e-mail but personal e-mail.

Too often overlooked is the other psychological component of e-mail marketing: Make response simple. Make it easy. Make it uncomplicated.

In the first instance, don't ask for even one bit more information than you need. Information greed has killed many a response in embryo.

Unless you have a marketing reason to remove yourself from the rapport arena, write within the experiential background of the reader, not yourself. Obviously, if you (or whoever writes your e-mail) and the reader share experiential backgrounds, communication should connect well. But don't throw around terms based on what you know and what the reader may not know. The medium is far past reader awe at getting a commercial e-mail message.

A simple psychological trick that usually works is assumptive sharing of experiential background. The writer words the message as though it is to someone he or she already knows. The reader joins the assumption. This trick can be tricky, because it usually is first name to first name, and the message dare not border on insult or invasion of privacy. It must be complimentary, stroking without the technique becoming an obvious sales ploy.

Quickly and constantly remind your target of your relationship.

Don't forget to thank them, no matter what. When a new name appears on your list, send an e-mail thank you. When a customer reorders, send a thank-you confirmation. When an e-mail question or complaint comes through, reply quickly and be sure to thank the individual for calling the matter to your attention.

Sometimes an apparently personal reply isn't possible. The rule is to hew as closely as possible to apparent personalization, remembering that most of your competitors won't do that—and, possibly more significantly, that a complaint aimed directly at you is better for your business and less likely to result in a lost customer than a complaint aimed outside.

Keep replies to e-mail from customers or prospects brief but friendly. And always reconfirm the customer's e-mail address.

The Pros and Cons of Passwords

E-marketers regard passwords as symbols of exclusivity—or, more crassly, symbols of online visitors having paid for information. But many online visitors regard passwords, even when the necessity is clear, as hair shirts.

This was an actual password for a newsletter that, curiously, had not demanded any input or money prior to issuance:

OiRd15

Now, who in perdition would be expected to remember that? The sequence of letters and numbers may have significance within the issuer's offices. To the user, it's obfuscatory . . . and obfuscation is the sworn enemy of both clarity and rapport.

Suggestion: If the dynamics and economics of your e-mails demand passwords, either have the individual choose his or her own password or offer passwords that have some mnemonic value.

The Value of Segmentation

A subject line that asks, "Kids going to college?" is a good headline only when you know your targets are parents of sixteen- to eighteen-year-olds. If you're shotgunning, the wastage can be devastating.

It becomes increasingly obvious that realized value comes from specific targeting. Ethnic lists let you say, "You and I are brothers," which means rapport . . . unless you seem patronizing. Executive lists make possible a mogul-to-mogul communication. Marketing to seniors, as explained earlier in this book, opens possibilities that are marginal when aimed at other groups.

Individual psychological ploys may require the professional laying on of hands, but the combination of segmentation and the knowledge of how to generate multiple targeted appeals already has proved its worth.

TIP

The classic marketing truth, *emotion outpulls intellect,* is as valuable a sales weapon as any e-marketer can aim.

Include a Call to Action

Millions of commercial e-mail messages soar serenely through the ether without ever landing.

The sender forgets one of the Great Laws of marketing: Tell the message recipient what to do.

Figure 6-5 doesn't have that problem. This example uses basic English, including inadvertent grammatical mistakes, to reach a specific level of online readership and attention. It has a primitive strength because of its carnival-pitch type of vernacular wording. Does it work? Only the sender has the answer to that question; but the possibility of getting response from those in need of this relief is higher than would be the case if the e-mail had been more formal.

Figure 6-5. Saying it like it is.

Subj:	**Secret's To Make Thousands Online! vusax**
Date:	9/21 3:41:45 AM Eastern Daylight Time
From:	lojeheyi@lanoce.com
Reply-to:	lojeheyi@lanoce.com
To:	gryzph@aol.com

heyi@lanoce.com

Earn $1783.00 or more per week

This offer is limited to the First 49 People Who Contact Me Today!
If you are tired of all the empty promises of money-making schemes, you're in Luck! We have weeded out the scams and shams and have found the best opportunities available. You can "truly" be making $100's, $1000's or more in extra cash a month. How does that sound? If you liked the sound of that, then how about this? You do not have to pay one dime to find out about these true money-making opportunities. Just click here and we will show you the best, "real" moneymakers available. It is absolutely 100% FREE, so visit us today, don't miss out on a real opportunity!

A message that doesn't include a call to action actually frustrates the recipient: "Why are they telling me this?" Chest-thumping and image-advertising are at odds with the implicit nature of this medium. The surname of e-mail is mail. Mail is supposed to be informative; but marketing mail should have a marketing purpose. Check every message to be sure you've included a call to action. Tell them to do something, even if it's just a "Click here for . . ." semi-instruction.

The All-Important Subject Line

Clichés Don't Hack It

How many e-mails do you get that seem to have the same subject line? Some infernal machine seems to be grinding these out like hamburger:

- Save on your auto insurance!

- Make millions by . . .

- Reach for the stars!

- New tool for . . .

- Free cash, never repay!

Yes, these do have the seeds of two essential elements: self-improvement and personal profit. But those seeds have been planted so many times that they have mutated into weeds.

Oddly, two of the most common clichés still work: *free* and *first time offered*. Variations on these two themes can stimulate response as no straightforward announcement ever could. One example of a substitute for *free* is: "If I hear from you by midnight tomorrow, this won't even cost you a dime." An example of a substitute for *first time offered* is: "This is all exclusively yours, not available to even one outsider, until midnight tomorrow."

Thinking in terms of an emotional reaction will do much to help create an inviting subject line. "New weapon for . . ." is far stronger than "New tool for . . ." and "I have the solution" is infinitely better than "Bad credit? The solution may be here."

(Chapter 10 and Chapter 11 discuss opening lines in considerable detail.)

TIP

An expiration date always helps response.

Names Have Power

In over 90 percent of tests, including the recipient's name in the subject line increases response. This is far beyond being a parallel to computerized personalization of a sales letter, because of the superior one-to-one nature of e-mail.

Should you use first name only or both first name and surname? Rules are slowly formulating. Younger people seem to like first names; older people may regard being addressed by their first name as an intrusion.

Some of the frequently visited sites, such as online auctions, use first name for multibuyers only, thinking—quite correctly in most cases—that this enhances rapport by assuming a posture of familiarity.

Current technology makes it surprisingly easy to include the city as well as the individual's name. Where the message itself makes a city reference logical, including this information usually gives yet another boost to response.

TIP

Don't extend specificity to inclusion of the recipient's postal code in an e-mail solicitation. Many who harbor no negative thoughts about seeing their town in the subject line react negatively to a postal code, which implies: "These people have investigated me."

Test, Test, Test!

Testing always has been the key to direct response success, and in e-mail, the significance of this procedure is amplified.

The reason, as touched on in the previous chapter, is that we have the most psychologically sensitive medium ever developed. But we're operating at a distance. The phrase "Little words mean a lot" was never more apt.

Add to this the ease of e-mail testing and we have no reason not to test.

The most logical test is that of subject line. Here is an example of an e-mail. The subject line:

Fortunes Being Made with New Product

The body copy begins:

The word is out! Oprah Winfrey is talking about it. Women are talking to other women about it. Men and women are making fortunes with it from their homes, right now today!

In that day's e-mail, the very next message has this subject line:

Baby Boomers Cashing In On Fortune-Making Trend!

The body copy of this e-mail begins:

The word is out! Oprah Winfrey is talking about it. Women are talking to other women about it. Men and women are making fortunes with it from their homes, right now today!

What is being sold? The only explanation is that it's a product "every adult man and woman wants," and one has to "Click here" to find out.

Obviously, this is a subject line test. Which one won? Only the sender knows. That sender has another nugget in his or her information base.

Business-to-Business May Have Different Rules

Two arguments, both equally logical, pertain to sending e-mail to business targets.

The first argument says these are people, and people respond *as people.* So stiffening the rhetoric, making it cold and humorless, is out of key with the desire to establish rapport—a goal as valid in business-to-business e-mail as it is in business-to-consumer e-mail.

The second argument says the ambience is different. Your target is sitting at a desk, beset with problems or projects, all of which are geared to timing. The mind-set rejects messages that seem to intrude on the businesslike attitude.

But there is a third factor: management attitude.

Some critics label the stringent no-nonsense approach to e-mail that some companies not only advocate but also enforce as "The Joke Police." An e-mailer may use a joke of the day as the vehicle on which to hang commercial messages. Uh-oh! A supervisor sees a joke on an employee's computer screen. The employee is labeled a laggard.

This attitude can extend to newsletters and other vehicles that are just that—vehicles. Since the attitude exists, mailers to lower or middle management should be aware of it.

In fact, software developers such as SurfControl, Baltimore Technologies, and Elron market software that scans both incoming and outgoing e-mail, blocking what it regards not only as spam, obscenity, or data that shouldn't leave the company's intranet but also jokes—any keywords or phrases the company's joke police select.

No question about it, an employer has the right to filter out corporate information that should be kept confidential. But e-mail is only one avenue for such information to escape. Sharing drinks at a local pub is an even more common vehicle.

A more logical apology for what might seem to be draconian measures exists: A company's computers are company property, and employees using that property are subject to company rules.

Probably an inevitable solution lies somewhere in the middle, where employees don't feel penalized and employers don't feel their computers are being used for either sabotage or for entertainment on company time.

Meanwhile, according to the American Management Association, an increasing number of companies each year monitor employee e-mail.

Knowing Who the Message Is From

The subject line is not identical to the sender line. From whom is this message? Two killers lurk in the very first few words.

If the recipient doesn't recognize the sender or the sender's type of business, suspicion begins. If nonrecognition is paired with what appears to be a pitch, the finger on the mouse twitches. Shazam! You're gone.

Using an individual's name as the "From" source can be a saving idea. People respond to people more than they do to corporations or fund-raisers.

Garbage Is in the Eye of the Beholder

A logical procedure is to send your e-mail to yourself before shot-gunning it.

This was an actual subject line:

Subj: **RE: Ïðîãðàìíîãîîïîààñïîðìñä÷àíèÿ** *http://moneysoft.sail.to*

What reaction could any recipient possibly have other than either frustration ("I guess my computer can't read this") or disgust ("I guess whoever sent this speaks Urdu")?

A Message Written in Crayola

A heavily reported early e-mail test was one mounted in 2000 by Binney & Smith, maker of Crayola crayons.

Crayola and its consultant, Mercer Management, developed a grid of seventy-two messages. From that core, the company tested sixteen e-mail greetings, all of which had as its goal getting people to visit Crayola.com, the company's Web site. Some individuals received messages almost generic in their approach, such as "Help us help you." Others were sent an incentive such as the possibility of a gift certificate. According to the company, the runaway winner was a "Crayola Survey" that included the first name of the recipient. The survey resulted in a 34 percent click-through to the site, an almost unheard-of response.

As more message senders realize the rapport-inducing value of name inclusion, percentages will drop because uniqueness disappears. Still, for now, the superiority of name inclusion remains unchallenged.

Verbs, Nouns, Adverbs, Adjectives, and Other Parts of Speech

Which part of speech has the greatest power? Nouns? Verbs? Adjectives? Adverbs? Prepositions?

Action comes from verbs. Imperatives come from verbs. Verbs have greater power than nouns, so when structuring subject lines, the verb—if you include one, and announcement-type subject lines may not—demands the greatest amount of attention.

For example, suppose you want someone to visit a store. Look at the huge assortment of imperative options available to you. Here are only a few, to give you an idea:

- Visit your nearest store.

- Walk to your nearest store.

- Run to your nearest store.

- Go to your nearest store.

- Get to your nearest store.

- Meander over to your nearest store.

- Drop in at your nearest store.

- Hurry to your nearest store.

- Zip over to your nearest store.

- Beat your feet to your nearest store.

On demand, you easily can add twenty more possibilities. You can see how long the list can be—and how many choices exist for you as a force-communicator. So the choice of verbs is crucial for an effective subject line.

Does safety lie in blandness? Not for e-mail. The Great Law of telling the target-individual what to do is a major player in convincing that person to read beyond the subject line.

Suppose an e-mail message has this subject line:

Information you should have about home improvement schemes

The subject line begins with a bland, neutral noun. Consider the same message when headed by a power verb:

Beware of home improvement schemes.

Does the message suffer because the word *information* is missing? You think so only if you believe *information* has the motivational power the imperative *beware* has.

Concentrating on verbs is usually a sound marketing decision. But even though well-chosen verbs have strength, other parts of speech can be valuable. The old standby from book titles and magazine articles, "How to . . ." can be effective; but unless "How to . . ." is followed by a power verb such as *win* or *beat* or *get rid of* or *dump* or *grab*, this opening drops into second place. Following "How to . . ." with *improve* or *fix* or *supervise* or *know* or *be* or *go* results in a vanilla flavor that can't compete with a power-verb first word.

Adverbs have greater e-mail power than adjectives, but they may be overlooked because attention to adjectives is … well, it's easier. Switching attention from adjectives to adverbs is a tricky proposition, always worth testing. The simplest test is using the same word, but adding an "-ly" suffix: *beautiful* becomes "beautifully" and *careful* becomes "carefully."

Why is adverb-testing a solid concept? Because adverbs seem more directly related to action. This is a minor point, but when sending tens of thousands of messages in which the subject line is the determinant of readership, minor points become major points.

TIP

Advertising is adjectival. Advertising writers look for adjectives and often subordinate the other parts of speech. Unless you want your message to reflect an advertising intent, play down the adjectives.

When appealing to vertical interest groups, a single noun can be effective: "Golf!" "Lover!" "Prostate!"

Why would the word *lover* be more effective than *love*? The word *love* is both noun and verb, and can't build a fast dramatic image the way the word *lover* can.

Some nouns, such as *loan* and *money*, have become so overused their impact is nominal. *Future* is a word without much impact in a subject line because of e-mail's aura of immediacy.

The most valuable e-mail noun is a proper noun—the individual's name. Depending on volume, software, and available data, you may or may not be able to include the name in the subject line. Not having it won't kill you, but including the name invariably improves response.

What if you don't have the actual name and have only the online name? Should you use that pseudonym in the subject line?

Certainly. It may be even more personal to the recipient than the actual name, and it includes the safety factor of moderately preserved anonymity. Tests are muddy here, but their very muddiness suggests possible value in testing online names against actual names.

Using Imperative vs. Declarative

One of the Great Laws of force-communication is: Tell the reader what to do.

This suggests that an imperative statement—such as "Do that" or "Don't do that"—has greater force than a declarative statement—such as "This is what successful operators do" or "Successful operators seldom do this." An additional advantage to an imperative is that it usually begins with a verb; a disadvantage is that verbs such as *do* or *see* or *look* are usually relatively colorless, compared with less-hackneyed imperatives.

So verb choice can be the difference between a ho-hum response and a barnburner. "Talk to me" can pull eight to ten times the response "Do me a favor" might generate.

The subject line in Figure 7-1 makes a strong promise the text doesn't fulfill. Without an example to back up the subject line, the message is flat.

Figure 7-1. An unfulfilled promise.

Subj:	**Joe, Great New Car Deals on the Net**
Date:	7:27:39 PM Pacific Daylight Time
From:	CarFinderNetwork-VYZ@msn.com

LOWEST Price On A New Car
WITHOUT Negotiating For Hours!

Skip the sales professional
that has to "Check with his manager"!
Get a FAST SEARCH Click Here

* **Prices based on dealer invoice.**
* **Latest Auto Price Search Engine does all the work.**
* **No aggravation.**
* **Save time.**
* **All brands, take your pick.**

Compare this message with the competing e-mail in Figure 7-2.

Figure 7-2. A motivational message.

Subj:	**HGLEWIS1, Find the lowest price on your new car or truck!** **jt dltxf fem khqt qr o**
Date:	6:05:06 PM Pacific Daylight Time
From:	carol217bjv@msn.com (Carol Rice)
Reply-to:	carol217bjv@msn.com
To:	hglewis1@aol.com

HGLEWIS1,

Looking for the best price on a new car or truck?

No cost! No obligation! No negotiating! Just one click away...

CLICK HERE to start your search!

_____

Your screen name of HGLEWIS1 is subscribed to our list.
To be removed from future offers, please click here.

_____

Does this subject line in Figure 7-2 seem more motivational than the one in Figure 7-1? Or would a statement of superiority, a warning, or an imperative—such as "Grab a new car at a ridiculous price" or "If you pass this up you're paying too much"—result in more click-throughs?

No rule is absolute. Claiming that imperatives always outpull declaratives ignores the invariable revelation stemming from dogged and intelligent testing. This is especially true since secrets—especially secrets related to response—last for only moments on the Web, and a flood of imperatives unleashes the sameness = boredom syndrome.

Ask a Question

Questions are automatically reader involving, and that benefit makes questions a logical testing procedure for e-mail.

The potential problem with questions is the possibility that the reader may find a particular question irrelevant or insulting. So for online purposes, safety lies in either asking provocative questions the reader cannot regard as irrelevant or insulting, or avoiding this potential minefield.

Some of the tested and successful questions we use in direct mail have produced only so-so results in e-mail—for example, questions replacing "Do you . . ." with the motivation-generating "Don't you . . ."

Compare the rhetorical strength of these three parallel openings:

1. You should . . .

2. Should you . . .

3. Shouldn't you . . .

That last entry combines question, provocation, challenge, and suggestion, and should produce greater response than either of the others. But test.

Because questions should have considerable motivational force, whenever possible test questions against the same subject line presented as a declarative statement.

Do little words mean a lot? Ha! They easily can mean the difference between success and failure.

Personalization and Relevance

If relevance is king, then assumptive rapport is the crown prince.

Long before the World Wide Web existed, direct mail had proved the point made conclusively in Chapter 6: Relevance is more significant than personalization.

For e-mail, many software packages provide personalized drop-ins. These often are indicated in the text as *$text$*—an indication of the place to drop in the name.

Because e-mail is a deliberately informal medium, using a person's first name only is the usual personalization. This is *assumptive rapport*, and unless the message itself is a mismatch, assumptive rapport is effective e-mail marketing.

A Necessary Disclaimer

I don't think anyone can tabulate the number of procedures, software packages, and take-charge organizations dedicated to improving e-mail image, response, and loyalties.

There are two reasons why this is so. First, e-mail is the hottest mass-marketing medium going. The bandwagon is big, wide, and inviting, and it is both natural and logical for a marketer with a bright idea—or a technician with a bright idea—to hop aboard that bandwagon.

Second, the bandwagon is crowded, and those near the edge can be thrown off and disappear. It's entirely possible that between the time I write this warning and the time you read it, many new possibilities will have sprung up and many others will have perished—even including some discussed in this chapter.

So under no circumstances should any reader regard these corporate vignettes as a complete listing. Rather, regard them as representative of what exists, plus a mild prediction of what may exist at a later date. These descriptions are reports, not recommendations. If companies that sell e-mail solutions want recommendations, let them write their own books.

Looking Glass and Cohorts

Developed by Looking Glass, located in Denver, Cohorts is a method of addressing demographic specifics the company describes as "a *household*-level (not neighborhood-based) market segmentation system. And that makes all the difference because it helps you target the right *households,* not just *neighborhoods*. Cohorts allows you to identify distinct customer groups within your customer file." (Examples of Cohorts appear in Chapter 5.)

Cohorts divides U.S. households into twenty-seven cohesive groups that share distinct demographic and lifestyle characteristics. Each group is given a Cohorts name, designed to reflect the way that name implies a personality, as distinguished from others. For example, married online customers might range from Alec and Elyse (affluent empty nesters) to Rodd and Tammie (a young family). Messages are segmented and targeted specifically at each set of demographic/psychographic characteristics.

The benefit to the nontechnical e-mail marketer is the ability to identify customer types as individuals, not as mere clusters of data, and to reach out to them with personalized messages and programs.

The three key benefits, according to Looking Glass, are:

1. Consumer segmentation creates large groups of households "that are homogenous with regard to lifestyles and behavior. So the impression of one-to-one marketing—actually 'one-to-some' marketing—sends the same customized and most relevant messages to those within an entire group of prospects or customers, on a highly cost-effective basis."

2. This technique strikes a perfect balance between the marketer's need for accurate targeting and the consumer's desire to protect his or her individual privacy. For example, a particular group's income and age can vary over wide ranges, but knowing that an individual belongs in a particular group does not permit the marketer to identify that individual's specific income or age.

3. Segmentation is independent of geography and does not assume that every member of a given neighborhood is similar in tastes and behavior. For example, having a young couple with three kids down the block with an elderly, retired couple next door questions the supposed homogeneity of neighborhoods.

In addition, Cohorts points out, how does geography relate to who is online?

Additional claimed benefits are that results are constant from product to product and application to application, and the method is sufficiently varied in its twenty-seven groups to account for the growing population diversity.

Equilibrix

Equilibrix is a Florida permission-based e-mail marketer. Noncompeting participating vendors share their e-mail databases, sending offers to those who have opted to receive information.

Customers at a retail store or other available location enter their e-mail addresses into an electronic data collector. The addresses are sent to and added to the Equilibrix database. Registered individuals then receive e-mail promotions designed by Equilibrix on behalf of the company's participating marketers.

This e-mail marketer aims the greater part of its e-mails at existing customers, since primary registration is at a business location.

Opt In Inc.

Opt In Inc. is a principal exponent of cost-per-action (CPA) as a replacement for cost-per-thousand (CPM).

Opt In has two CPA networks: the Opt In Network and the CPA Distribution Network. Both are based on performance-based media buying. The company says its success is tied to online visitor attitude, which is self-centered and without much loyalty to vendors, making return on investment (ROI) the most dependable litmus test for e-mail marketing. Sales literature points out that "in a no-loyalty environment, ROI is king," with reference to a report from Forrester Research showing a considerable anticipated increase of CPA marketing over CPM marketing.

Opt In Inc. offers marketers CPA with no set-up fees for tracking or integration, short-term deals with escape clauses, and "carefully chosen lists instead of indiscriminate shotgunning."

Presenter.com

Presenter.com licenses rich media software. One product is called *iPresentation Maker*, a presentation-authoring tool that combines video with PowerPoint slides.

According to the company, *iPresentation Maker* can import slides from PowerPoint, include streaming audio/video, and with reasonable speed create online presentations paralleling those the viewer might see and hear when attending a speech.

Another Presenter.com rich media product is *Instant Presentation*. This program enables senders "to view reports that track who has opened the Presentations and what portions were viewed"—a next-generation benefit that goes beyond standard e-mail. Message recipients can view the presentations by using established Internet Media player standards, such as Windows Media™ Player and RealPlayer®."

The company points out that its system is unusually useful for generating corporate communications because of the speed with which presentations can be mounted or revised.

Are these presentations e-mail or are they designed to upgrade standard PowerPoint presentations and offer an alternative to video-conferencing? To quote the company's sales literature: "iPresentations . . . include video, audio, a linkable table of contents, and PowerPoint slides. Presenters upload their presentations and use the phone to record narrations. Attendees are sent an e-mail message containing the Web address of the presentation; RealNetworks' RealPlayer or Windows Media Player is required for viewing."

Accucast

Accucast is an e-mail marketing software system produced by a company named Socketware, Inc. Accucast runs on a Java-enabled Web server. According to Socketware sales literature, Accucast enables organizations to launch permission-based e-mail marketing campaigns that "generate high response rates, increase revenue, and build strong customer relationships." Accucast includes customization and personalization features that deliver media-rich content.

Accucast is currently available in three forms: *Enterprise, Accelerator,* and *Agency. Enterprise* has the capability of sending millions of messages per hour without requiring new hardware. It is fully scalable, running on most systems, including Windows NT/2000 and Unix.

Enterprise interacts with database information, allowing the sender to deliver messages tailored to users' preferences, including embedding content from any Web page or application into the e-mail message—newsletters, account statements, press releases, or banner advertisements.

According to Socketware, Accucast's *Accelerator* "lets you design and deliver targeted, personalized, direct e-mail marketing campaigns right from your desktop without IT involvement." *Accelerator's* interface enables an e-marketer to send customized communications to customers and prospects, develop one-to-one relationships, and learn about buying habits and preferences, without new hardware or extra staff. Accelerator captures click-throughs and collects data about those who respond, which is valuable in interpreting market behavior.

Accucast's *Agency*, says Socketware, delivers targeted e-mails at low cost, in either plain text or HTML e-mail content, including streaming media. The program automatically detects which recipients can receive HTML messages.

Socketware offers the option of in-house messaging or sending the information to the company for hosting data and powering the messaging.

Ascendant Media

Ascendant Media is a promotions and sweepstakes company that profiles entrants by the type of sweepstakes they enter. The company claimed that one e-mail campaign targeting members of a sweepstakes site who had shown an interest in financial services resulted in an online broker signing more than 400 new accounts.

The company has a sweepstakes called Ezsweeps. According to information on the Web site, online visitors can be entered automatically in the sweepstakes they select from Ascendant Media's Lucky's Sweeps page and add it to their My Sweeps page. Each day the individual revisits the site, Ascendant automatically reenters that person in all sweeps "for which you are eligible for reentry. If you then choose to enter a new sweepstakes, you need only click on the entry button on that sweep and it will be added to your EZsweeps Personal Portfolio."

Video E-Mail

Video e-mail is a virtual TV system, used primarily for Web site imagery. But the company recruits its audiences by sending e-mails that include a video sample. The procedure also enhances e-mail transmissions.

Video e-mail delivers streaming video programs by e-mail at specific intervals. Users sign up for channels they want sent to their e-mail addresses, and transmission is effected either by modem or by broadband.

Responsys

Responsys is an e-mail marketing system headquartered in Palo Alto, California. The company claims to lower the cost of customer acquisition "from around $100 for web banner ads or $40 for direct mail pieces to just $5 for permission-based marketing."

The Responsys.com Interact system is intended to increase customer loyalty "by providing personalized e-mail campaigns that are dynamically assembled according to your customer's interests and/or personal data and location. Therefore, an increase in revenue will result from greater conversion rates and the ability to cross-sell, for example." Responsys.com allows the marketer to respond rapidly to change by viewing e-mail marketing tracking and click-through results in real time. Thus, the marketer can modify e-mail marketing campaigns instantly.

Responsys offers five service options:

1. Campaign services allow the marketer to define, test, and manage campaigns.

2. Launch services allow the marketer to deliver high-volume personalized campaign messages to consumers.

3. Response services allow the marketer to collect data from consumers responding to campaigns, either using prefilled call-to-action forms or click-through URL links. The response

services also handle consumer requests to opt out of mailing lists or requests to update user profiles.

4. Data services allow the marketer to import, export, and manage mailings lists, profile tables, response tables, campaign messages, and forms, plus connect and extract data to and from data tables external to the system.

5. Image services allow the marketer to stage and serve up images that are included in HTML-based campaign messages.

CyBuy

New York–based CyBuy says its approach to e-mail transactions is based on a Harris Interactive survey the company commissioned. The survey, CyBuy says, showed that 62 percent of online shoppers would complete a purchase transaction if they could do so directly from the e-mail screen—a conclusion in sync with the impulse-reaction typical of online activity.

CyBuy provides embedded order forms for e-mail and also has a technology that allows consumers to buy merchandise and services directly through their television sets.

Dynamics Direct

Dynamics Direct is a California company specializing in rich media e-mail.

The company advertises that it "offers a full suite of e-mail messaging solutions that meet your customer lifecycle needs." The core is a trademarked technology called D.R.I.V.E.—Dynamic Rich Individualized E-mail. According to a sales brochure, D.R.I.V.E. "seamlessly and automatically customizes each rich media e-mail message for each recipient based on client database information and real-time user input."

Dynamics Direct's system enables the recipient to conduct a transaction without leaving the e-mail message.

DoubleClick

DoubleClick Inc. has a proprietary technology called DART. DART-mail Campaign Manager, the company says, offers advertisers "a full service campaign management solution for direct e-mail marketing. This solution enables marketers to deliver highly personalized e-mail communications to their existing customers and helps merchants build their customer lists and facilitate outbound communications."

The company's offerings are segmented. Examples: DART for Advertisers; DART for Publishers; and AdServer, an inventory and order management, targeting, delivery, tracking, and campaign reporting service.

DoubleClick is both a list manager and a list broker. At press time, the company claims exclusive management of 19 million online addresses and brokerage of 50 million online addresses.

TIP

When renting names, insist on the same merge-purge privileges that extend to names rented for direct mail. One individual may not only have three or four online addresses but also be carried on numerous lists.

Naviant

According to its sales literature, Naviant is the source of Wired Mail, a "suite of digital products that leverages the depth and breadth of the High Tech Household database to create a full e-mail marketing tool set." Wired Mail includes three complementary e-mail products: *WiredMail Prospector*, *WiredMail Append*, and *WiredMail Manager*.

WiredMail Prospector is an e-mail list rental property, including e-mail and postal address, demographic, geographic, behavioral, and interest data. *WiredMail Append* is an enhancement process the company says adds these dimensions to rented names for e-mail solicitation: reducing costs through online channel; building a loyalty/retention program; making special, time-sensitive offers; enhancing customer serviceability; accelerating campaign testing cycles; driving site-based revenue opportunities; and adding an additional customer touchpoint.

Wired Mail Manager handles message creation and management.

Inceptor Excedia

According to its sales literature, Excedia's e-mail communication functionality:

> *Enables marketers to manage e-mail campaigns by leveraging the content visibility, tracking, and analysis capabilities offered through the application. It is designed to integrate your Web resources and e-mail campaigns into an effective and efficient marketing tool. You will be able to create one-to-one e-mail marketing campaigns that integrate existing e-mail and customer resources to existing Web resources.*

Excedia's e-mail communication includes a customer retention tool that "refines the quality of repeat customer traffic to your Web site, thus improving the conversion to sale rate for your marketing campaigns."

Typical uses of Excedia's e-mail communication feature are:

- Extracting customer and prospect details from a database

- Setting up Web page links to be sent to customers

- Entering campaign details, including e-mail details

- Sending e-mail requests to local e-mail server

- Sending e-mails to customers and prospects via Excedia's local e-mail server

- Ensuring customer/prospect receives personalized e-mail

- Redirecting customers/prospects instantly to an existing Web page when they click on a URL provided in e-mail that connects to the Excedia server

- Recording in a log the fact that the customer/prospect clicked on the URL sent in the e-mail

- Providing the marketer views of the tracking information and statistics on the e-mail campaign

- Feeding results from the e-mail campaign back into the database for subsequent e-mail campaigns

Charting What Is State of the Art

These are just a few random examples of what is out there. The samples and descriptions are in no way intended to be either complete or an endorsement of any particular product.

Companies constantly open, close, and shift both product and emphasis. Use this quick list to get the flavor of what is out there. By the time you read this, one of these suppliers—or dozens of others—may have introduced software or procedures that make every one listed in this chapter obsolete.

A wonderful and frustrating facet of e-mail marketing is that it's *alive*. It lives, breathes, and grows by the hour—like a science-fiction monster. Or more aptly, it's like a mutant superspecies, destined to outpace what we once thought was state of the art.

Holding On to Fragile Response

We all have seen entertainers who don't entertain, lecturers who bore their audiences, and celebrities whose thin façade of sophistication wears off quickly under the modest heat of an interview. They struggle uncomfortably on the stage or in front of the camera, wondering what is wrong with their audience.

The problem isn't with the audience. The audience tuned in or paid admission or showed up. They weren't negative . . . originally. Are they to blame because they don't find the comedian funny, the lecture useful, or the celebrity worth seeing?

That magical word *rapport* (see Chapter 5) is missing. Some people never can find it because they don't have the foggiest notion how to generate it.

Look at the message in Figure 9-1. Does it generate rapport, or defy it? This message came from an unknown source. Many recipients will open it out of curiosity or the powerful human motivator of

Figure 9-1. Does this message generate rapport?

Subj:	**Here ya go sis:)**
Date:	4:52:51 PM Pacific Standard Time
From:	jennifer_cornell_2000@dunya.onar.com.tr (Jen)
To:	Cris429@dunya.onar.com.tr

hey sis,
this is the Martial art and Personal protection
site i bought the nunchucks and the tazer from.
you guys going to be ontime sunday????
Martial art and Personal protection
Cris

voyeurism. The response that results depends on whether the message generates rapport.

Those people shouldn't write e-mail messages.

Nor should the bookkeeper who has designed the online shopping cart to which a successful e-mail message has delivered a prospect. Does this bookkeeper have any knowledge of sales psychology? If not, retain the bookkeeper role and stay out of marketing.

The percentage of orders that collapse *after* the prospect has reached the shopping cart is nothing short of ghastly—proof that a knowledge of bookkeeping and a knowledge of sales psychology are not always embodied in the same person.

Who Are You?

A Web site sits, like a city, waiting for visitors. Note the similarities: Visitors come to the city. They can dawdle in the park or head straight to the downtown shopping areas.

An e-mail message is like an airplane bringing an unexpected visitor to the prospect. Note the circumstance: The airplane lands on the prospect's runway, as many other planes are beckoning for a landing.

Certainly, that magical word *rapport* applies to both circumstances. But the sales psychology can't be the same, despite the plethora of articles and speeches lumping all facets of the World Wide Web into one psychological bucket.

Sequence: "Here's my order. Hmm. Aw, forget about it." Why is a horrendous percentage of orders disappearing at the exact moment they shouldn't disappear—just when the customer is at the virtual checkout counter?

Three possible faults exist. The first—and most common—fault is demanding more information than the individual has either the time or the inclination to give up. Technology should be sufficiently effective for placing the ordered item in position. Now, how about personal information?

Have you, as vendor, offered a benefit—such as a bonus, a gift, a discount, or a Gold Card membership—a *something*, for preregistration? Have you issued a password that identifies the person and automatically puts name and address on the order form? Why not?

TIP
_____

If you require a password, ask yourself why. Customers know they don't need a password to order from a printed catalog or to shop in a store. Why do they need a password from you? Give them a reason that seems to benefit them, not you.

_____

Assuming your customer doesn't have a prelisted password that eliminates many of the fill-ins, both logic and sales expertise tell you to keep those fill-ins to a minimum. What do you need other than name, address, and charge-card information? If that is all, stop there until the order is complete. You can send e-mail later, asking peripheral questions. Or you can offer a post-confirmation bonus for additional information. For now, don't endanger the order.

The second fault is being so concerned with completeness that you drop your customer into an electronic maze. Suppose the customer wants to change the quantity from one to two. How difficult have you made that little decision?

TIP

Why ask for city, state, and zip code, when the zip code alone tells you the city and state?

When a customer abandons the shopping cart right at the moment when the order is supposed to be complete, that is nothing short of criminal. It suggests you've demanded too much information, required too many click-throughs, or made navigation an adventure instead of a pleasure.

TIP

Don't be so in love with your home page that you constantly link e-mail to that page, regardless of what the specific offer might be. Send visitors where they want to go, not where you're happiest.

The third fault is the least excusable: "sticker shock." This comes from sudden arithmetic, added conditions, or disclaimers that add an impression of phoniness to your offer. This is no place for the kind of withdrawals for which you'd use an accursed asterisk in a space advertisement or direct-mail message. The psychology of effective e-mail is *straightforward one-to-one*. Violate that at your own peril.

If you have a subscription offer at forty-four cents per issue ("less than half the newsstand price"), covering five issues a week, for a year, it seems to be a terrific bargain until the moment of truth, when the subscriber sees 52 x 5 x .44 = $114.40. Will partial disclosure, blunting sticker shock ("You save more than $125!"), damage response or help prevent checkout bailout? I'd certainly test it.

TIP

Don't wait until the customer is in the shopping cart to disclose the price. That's not only a sign of cowardice, it's also stupid sales psychology.

A common cause of losing the order at "the moment of truth" is having the truth turn ugly by changing the original description or interpretation. Although you don't need to make a big deal of shipping costs, you shouldn't suddenly introduce conditions and exceptions, which add to skepticism. Later, no matter what you do, some customers will develop that disastrous syndrome, "Buyer's Remorse." Don't let it happen before the order is firm. How many shopping carts have _you_ abandoned when you see—suddenly—a hefty shipping charge that had no prior reference, not even a "plus nominal shipping charge"?

Peaceful Coexistence

Obviously, the World Wide Web and its giant offspring e-mail aren't going to drive other media out of business. Equally obvious, e-mail has chomped a huge chunk of advertising budgets away from other media. Is cannibalizing from one's own customer base a wasteful and ridiculous business practice?

Most astute marketers will answer quickly, "Absolutely not." Cannibalizing not only keeps a customer as a customer but also brings with it additional loyalty. And included in the mix will be previously unconverted inquiries, plus prospects who had been customers of other companies.

That same conclusion doesn't necessarily apply to advertising whose sole purpose is to drive people to the Web site. For example, catalogs certainly should offer the online option and, relative to e-mail rather than a passive Web site, suggest daily specials and hot-line closeouts, but not exist solely as an online feeder mechanism.

Bots

Bots are search mechanisms that cater to the basis for much Web marketing, which is price.

Most often, individuals will seek out a bot to get a price for a computer, a printer, a name-brand appliance, or any item whose price is likely to vary from one retailer to another. But bots, once they have your name, will use e-mail to solicit business. Figure 9-2 is an example of a typical e-mail message from a bot. In this case, the bot is MySimon, whose primary function is to search for competitive prices, although bots sometimes may include unsolicited e-mail.

Figure 9-2. Bots also send unsolicited e-mail.

Subj:	**mySimonSays: Get Great Gifts for Grads!**
Date:	3:37:46 PM Central Daylight Time
From:	mySimon_mySimonSays@postoffice.mysimon.com (mySimon)
To:	dragonelle@aol.com

Dear mySimon Shopper,

Check out our various shopping departments for more graduation gift ideas:

Consumer Electronics
Click here to shop
Computers
Click here to shop
Jewelry & Watches
Click here to shop

Happy Shopping!

_____

IN THIS ISSUE:

Graduation Gift Guide
Click here to view this page on the web

It's that time again. Time for marches to "Pomp and
Circumstance" and gleefully tossed mortarboards. Whether
the grad you're shopping for is a high school or college
student, a carefully chosen gift expresses admiration for
all of their hard work.

_____

For High School Grads

Under $50
Read More

$50 to $100
Read More

Over $100
Read More

_____

For College Grads

Under $50
Read More

$50 to $100
Read More

Over $100
Read More

_____

(continues)

Figure 9-2. (*continued*)

Love mySimon?

Then show your support by voting for us!

mySimon's been nominated for the 2001 Webby Award for Best Commerce Web Site. Click here to cast your vote.

Vote!

_____

Your email (dragonelle@aol.com) is on our mailing list. To unsubscribe, please forward this message to mailto:mySimon_mySimonSays Unsub@postoffice.mysimon.com and type "unsubscribe" in the body of the email. To subscribe, please forward this message to mailto: mySimon_mySimonSaysSub@postoffice.mysimon.com and type "subscribe" in the body of the email.

Motivate!

In the murky world of twenty-first century marketing, five major motivators sit waiting for the vendor to grasp and extend them. They are:

1. Fear

2. Exclusivity

3. Greed

4. Guilt

5. Need for approval

Nestled under these are two "soft" motivators, which can massage and aid the great five:

1. Convenience

2. Pleasure

Build your message around one of these motivators and chances for success increase exponentially. That's because you force the message to include a reason for response.

Figure 9-3 is an example of e-mail using *guilt* as the motivator. Although it isn't particularly strong, it's a message that would lose a great deal of impact if that motivator weren't there.

Figure 9-3. Using guilt to motivate.

Subj:	**Quality Time With Your Child...**
Date:	12:05:35 PM Pacific Daylight Time
From:	charlene_heart@yahoo.com (hearts&hugs)

How involved are you in your child's life?

Wouldn't you like to do something
that you would BOTH enjoy?
Look no further!

Our program was created to
encourage parents and children
to spend QUALITY time together!

Receive a FREE craft box and
supplies with a trial membership.

There is no obligation, no minimum
number of kits to buy, and you may
cancel anytime.

Get started TODAY!

Reply with your name, address,
and phone number.

Note the use of the word *free* in Figure 9-3. Does it help or hurt? The reason for this question is that in this circumstance, the word *free* takes the seventh veil off the offer and reveals it for what it is— a sales pitch.

E-Testing

Do you know what is pulling and what isn't? Which version of whatever is doing well and producing the most response?

You do if you test one item at a time.

Don't test price and message length at the same time. The results will be muddy. It also isn't a good idea to intermix any other element in a test of HTML against text. If you add another variable, the results will be muddy. Test one item at a time.

If you're testing motivators such as fear, exclusivity, greed, guilt, or need for approval, don't test any other element in the same message. But when you have a winner, you should *retest* with a second element, such as price. Why? Because greed may (and probably will) outpull any other motivator when the target individual perceives a bargain to be the key. This may not be the winner when the thrust is "Only you" or "Look out."

A Logical Experiment

A Fairfax, Virginia-based company called Shop2U has developed *The Registration Program*, designed to help clients find better prospects via e-mail. *The Registration Program* allows clients to be included in a regular e-mail sent to members of the 1.2 million names in Shop2U's E-Catalog of the Week database. The company says consumers who click on one of the highlighted catalog covers in the e-mail receive an electronic version of that catalog within forty-eight hours.

Shop2U is testing a ride-along version of the program. In that version, e-mail customers of a specific catalog get a branded e-mail message ostensibly sent by that catalog. Along with products from that catalog is an invitation to continue to receive e-catalogs, plus offers from any one of four highlighted catalogs.

Confusing? Maybe, to some people. Effective? Maybe for others. If this procedure results in increased response without generating a high-irritation factor, it will survive.

Technological Experimentation

Macy's Direct, a subsidiary of Federated Department Stores, Inc., worked with CheetahMail, Inc., to prepare an HTML messaging capability.

The arrangement offers Macys.com customers who have indicated a willingness to receive e-mail-based offers (originally through America Online) the opportunity to see those e-mail messages in HTML.

A Noble Experiment

What might happen when a not-for-profit organization uses an unrelated list to raise funds, because the list is donated?

Probably, the result would be a belief that e-mail doesn't work for fund-raising.

E-mail certainly does work for fund-raising; but not when sent randomly or without some sort of logical tie to the organization.

The National Coalition for the Homeless sent 100,000 e-mails to BetterGolf.net subscribers. Why did they choose that list? Because, they said, "We had to find a list vendor that would be willing to donate a good portion of their list."

If many BetterGolf.net subscribers regarded e-mail from an unrelated not-for-profit group, one they hadn't heard of, as spam, they would be justified. A spokesperson for The National Coalition for the Homeless made this admission: "Granted, they're not people who necessarily expressed an interest. That's the only thing that's missing here, is that there are no fund-raisers or donors. There might be some in there, we just don't know. But volume was key."

These e-mails do great damage to the entire phylum of online fund-raising. To knowledgeable marketers, the statement, "Granted, they're not people who necessarily expressed an interest. That's the only thing that's missing here," is parallel to saying, "You didn't order oysters, but I'm serving them to you because the only thing missing is that you didn't order them."

Did the e-mail produce results? Information wasn't available. But even if it did, the procedure was wrong. The proper approach would have been for the list owner to send the appeal, based on whatever binder the creative team could invent.

A Rational Assumption

It's entirely rational to assume you should cross-sell or upsell when sending an e-mail acknowledging an order. This is the moment at which the customer is most receptive.

The one-click-of-the-mouse-will-add-this-benefit technique, built into an order acknowledgment, not only costs next to nothing but is a technique founded in centuries of sales expertise. Recognizing that the Web is, in general, price-driven, adds exclusivity to the mix: "Because you're you, you'll get this additional whatever at a special 20% discount. And we can bundle it right in with your order." That's three "you" references in a row, plus a lower price.

TIP

When emphasizing discount, it's "20%," not "20 percent." When the message is upscale or genteel, it's "twenty percent."

Be careful with that offer to bundle the upgrade or additional whatever in with the original order. This works only when you're positive the customer won't think the additional item will slow down the shipment.

Without Relevance, You Have No Relevance

That subhead may seem to be redundant, but it's intentionally so. Relevance is a major clue to generating e-mail response, and the notion that an e-mail that does little more than say to the reader, "I am the greatest," will produce response is more than faulty; it smacks of the naïveté generic to a state of mind that values self-reaction above Web visitor reaction.

An example of this redundancy is in Figure 9-4, an e-mail from a respected marketer who makes an erroneous assumption about the type of message the online visitor will welcome. Although it is well-produced and harmless, this e-mail accomplishes little as a positive public relations ploy because the recipient becomes irritated by the lack of specificity relative to him or her.

Figure 9-4. Subject line needs relevance for recipient.

Subj:	**Peet's Celebrates Coffee Freshness Week**
Date:	2:20:35 PM Central Standard Time
From:	PeetsNews@peets.m0.net (Peet's Coffee & Tea)
Reply-to:	PeetsNews@peets.m0.net
To:	dragonelle@aol.com

As professional as this e-mail is, does it have the impact it might have had if the heading had more relevance to the recipient? "Peet's Celebrates Coffee Freshness Week" may have some impact within the Peet's sales office; but to many outsiders, no matter how much they love coffee, it's trivia because relevance isn't revealed in this e-mail, which seems to be nothing but self-acclamation.

TIP

An absolute assumption any marketer should embrace: Bury your own ego. Revere and cater to your target's ego.

Words and Phrases That Work

How do you grab attention in an increasingly sophisticated market-place?

The answer is consistent with a blend of the following three elements:

1. Benefit

2. Rapport

3. Verisimilitude—the appearance of truth

E-mails that work—especially *unanticipated* e-mails—tend to include all three elements. Those with two elements still have a major chance of generating response. And you might think that even just one element makes success more likely than might be expected from a message that didn't lean on one of these three powerful underpinnings. But dependence on only one of the three elements can lead to a pleasant message that produces little response. Why?

The claim of benefit without accompanying verisimilitude is unbelievable, and readers will click away from it. Rapport without benefit is fine for a personal message but useless for a sales message. Verisimilitude exists to verify a claim, and if no claim is made, it's pointless.

If you accept the notion of rapport, you automatically accept the superiority of "I" over "We." The difference in receptivity isn't even measurable.

You also accept that "What's your opinion of this?" has higher octane than "What do you think of this?" because *opinion* is a more rapport-inducing word than the looser *think*. And consider the greater power that the phrase "Okay, where were you last night?" has over the same opening without the first word: "Where were you last night?"

In e-mail, the maxim *Every word is our weapon* has greater validity than in any other medium, including conversation. Why including conversation? Because one can temper conversation by using inflection. E-mail words stand or fall on their own.

Words That Always Work

Some words have automatic power. Obviously, that power is gradually fading as the Web underscores The Sameness Rule:

Sameness = boredom

Overuse = abuse

While they last, e-mailers can exploit this short list of "can't miss" words:

- Private
- Free

- Congratulations!

- Uh-oh!

- Nuts!

- Phooey

- Success!

- Blah

- Alert!

- Quick!

- Hot

And feel free to use any of these boilerplate openings:

- Hi, You may remember me, my name is Audrey. Our mutual friend asked me to write to you a few weeks ago . . .

- Did you ever know a man named Charley?

- You're going to lose this bet.

- Sorry, it's too late.

- Our relationship.

- AS SEEN ON NATIONAL TV:

- Let *[NAME]* pick his own gift.

- Take a sneak peek at . . .

- Read this ASAP.

- Look at this only if you . . .

- This is not adult content.

- Forgive me, for I have spammed.

- Need to collect a judgment on anyone?

- You'll be interested in this.

- I'm not supposed to tell you this.

- I meant to tell you this earlier.

- I could get fired for telling you . . .

- I'm going to brighten your day.

- I'm going to make you an offer you can't refuse. (NOTE: *not* "This is an offer you can't refuse.")

- You said you want this. Lucky you.

- If you have an HP printer, click here now.

- Remember me?

- I have a terrible time keeping a secret.

- Here's your discount.

- Private investment advisory.

- First announcement: new Web site.

- Sorry I missed you.
  I'm all yours.

- It's probably too late.

- Lover, when you're near me . . .

- Be glad you waited.

The following phrases work, but are of questionable ethics:

- You excite me.

- I have money for you.

- Bill thought you'd like this.

- Have you gotten your order yet?

- I know what you did last night.

- You and I are relatives.

- Congratulations! You get two free airline tickets.

- It's payback time.

- Re: Your potential request.

- Request number 434013.

- You haven't yet picked up your free gift.

- *[NAME]*, receive a FREE Neutrogena travel set and FREE standard shipping! *[to get free item requires purchase]*

- Thank you for entering.

- I feel sexy tonight.

A Few "Grabbers"

Figure 10-1, Figure 10-2, and Figure 10-3 contain the opening blasts—but not necessarily the complete message—of some unanticipated offers exactly as they were sent. If you aren't moved by these offers, you are remaining analytical, probably the proper posture when seeing them out of context.

They appear in this chapter not as editorial endorsements but only as examples of e-mails that combine the three elements of e-mail success.

Figure 10-1. Listen to the music.

Subj:	**Play your favorite MP3 files on your cassette player!—ClubMail/Etracks.com**
Date:	4/3/ 5:18:28 PM Pacific Daylight Time
From:	clubmail@response.etracks.com (ClubMail/Etracks.com)
To:	hot99@aol.com

PLAY YOUR FAVORITE MP3'S AND AUDIO BOOKS WITH THIS DIGITAL CASSETTE!
PLAY IN YOUR CAR, BOOMBOX, OR ANYWHERE THERE IS A CASSETTE DECK!
Digisette Duo-64
Get ready for the next chapter in digital music evolution!
Introducing the DUO-64 digital player from Digesette now new at
Etracks.com(tm). The DUO-64 digital player works as both a stand-
alone MP3 and digital audiobook player, and a digital E-cassette
you can play in your car . . . in a boombox . . . in any cassette player!
Only on Etracks.com(tm), you can find this versatile digital audio
player for only $269.95!

Figure 10-2. Free cash grants.

Subj:	**NEVER REPAY, FREE CASH GRANTS . . .**
Date:	4/4/ 6:43:12 AM Pacific Daylight Time
From:	mikeebey@top.igetcarter.com
Reply-to:	msef3fe5tw@yahoo.com
To:	tigger5735@aol.com
CC:	dscipl211@aol.com, do0rd1e@aol.com, chipsjsun1@aol.com, cshrimp-man@aol.com, ricodep@aol.com, rage767@aol.com, genort@aol.com,dflan44958@aol.com, hotshot949@aol.com

Dear Friend,

FREE CASH GRANTS, NEVER REPAY!

Figure 10-3. The key to your future.

Subj:	**A TRUE College Degree . . .The key to your future**
Date:	4/4/ 9:46:51 AM Pacific Daylight Time
From:	/ paulchen66@baybreez.com
To:	keo@aol.com

Subj: GO TO COLLEGE WITHOUT GOING TO CLASS!
It is no longer necessary to attend college in order to earn a college degree in business or nursing. Distance Education is the fast, inexpensive way to earn a quality, accredited college education without attending lifedisrupti college classes.

_____

CLICK HERE TO FIND OUT HOW!

_____

Who can resist the opening in Figure 10-4? (Then see what is wrong with the follow-up.)

Figure 10-4. It's all free.

ATTENTION: Herschell Lewis,

I have been instructed to contact you about a FREE cellular
telephone with FREE shipping and $60 CASH REBATE on reserve
for Herschell Lewis. Your Ericsson T19LX digital telephone
is a stateoftheart communications device that includes
FREE caller ID, FREE voice mail, FREE text messaging and
AT&T Wireless service with 1400 minutes included for only
$39.99 per month.

CLICK NOW!

What happens with this type of immediate disclaimer is a force-feed of the reader's implicit skepticism. This unusually potent opening needs two or three additional "stroking" sentences before launching into a hard pitch.

Now let's look at some more extended examples.

The word *congratulations*, although overworked, still can command attention. When using this word, ask yourself: Have I convinced the recipient that my congratulations are genuine and for a genuine reason? Figure 10-5 contains a typical "Congratulations!" e-mail, obviously bulk-sent because the address and the personalization don't match. Note that this requires a blind participation, which in this example is filling out a form.

Figure 10-5. Congratulations to the finalist.

Subj:	**Finalist Notification for gryphy q w jn kuisva b**
Date:	5:16:56 AM Pacific Daylight Time
From:	laurie077lsc@msn.com (Laurie Hayes)
Reply-to:	laurie077lsc@msn.com
To:	gryphy@aol.com

CONGRATULATIONS, TOUGHGUY!
You have been selected as a finalist in the NVP "Travel Today Giveaway"!
Prizes are accommodations for two for two nights at any one of the following locations:

— Ft. Lauderdale or Daytona, FL
— Williamsburg, VA
— Orlando, FL
— Las Vegas, NV
— Bahamas
— Branson, MO

All you have to do is complete the finalists' registration form - be sure to include your Confirmation Number: G-218588.

As an added bonus, the first 500 finalists to register will receive a free entry in one of our bonus drawings for $1,000.00 Cash or Plane Tickets for 4 Adults to any Continental U.S. Destination!

Why wait? You could be on your way! CLICK HERE to "Travel Today"!
Laurie Hayes
National Vacation Promotions

Your screen name toughguy was entered in our giveaway.
If you do not wish to participate in future promotions, please click here.

Now compare the congratulatory message of Figure 10-5 with the simplicity of the message in Figure 10-6.

Figure 10-6. You're a winner.

Subj:	**Congratulations: You're our winner, You won our prize! 2365**
Date:	2:59:55 AM Pacific Standard Time
From:	YouWon30DollarsToday_8285@yahoo.com

Dear Friend,

Out of 50 million Internet users our computer has selected as you as one of 2000 winners. The Online Casino Of The Year is giving you $30 FREE. Congratulations!
CLICK HERE TO COLLECT
YOUR MONEY NOW!

The $30 gift money can be used at any of our exciting live, online casino games. The $30 is real and so are the games. All you have

to do is become a player and you can start gambling with your
FREE $30 bonus.

_____

WAIT, there's more.
There's cash hidden under one of these boxes.

Click on the right box for an additional BONUS
[BOX 1] [BOX 2] [BOX 3]

_____

Duplicity damages every e-marketer. The message in Figure
10-7 calls itself a follow-up. Many recipients will begin reading
based on the belief that it represents a reply to an inquiry, which it
does not.

Figure 10-7. A misleading follow-up.

Subj:	**Follow-up on Confirmation number 380385**
Date:	9/1 6:15:59 PM Eastern Daylight Time
From:	an1absolem@gte.com (an1absolem@gte.com)
To:	6698@mailcity.com (6698@mailcity.com)
CC:	[long list of online addresses]

Give your family great program choices and save money!

Get up to 125 Channels of Cable/Digital TV with
NO monthly fees!

Quality family channels like Disney, History, Discovery, Cartoon Network, Lifetime,
and A&E.

Movie channels like HBO, Showtime, Starz, Cinemax and more.

Sports stations like ESPN, ESPN2 and many more.

Save on your cable/satellite now

Words and Phrases That Don't Work

A great many of the words and phrases that don't work in e-mail parallel words and phrases that don't work in other avenues of communication. For example:

- There is (or There are)

- Remember

- It (as a first word)

Some subject lines and headings fail because they too quickly synopsize the selling argument. For example, suppose a subject line reads: "Increase Sales, Accept Credit Cards." Although completely descriptive, the line suffers from two problems. First, and easiest to correct, are the initial caps—capitalizing each word—which quickly brands the message as advertising. Second, a subject line as simple as "Increase sales" is an improvement; "Increase your sales" ties the message to the reader; "How to increase your sales" goes yet another step; "Shouldn't you increase your sales?" is challenging and involving.

Many words and phrases fail because they're wrong for the specific message. Many more fail because the writer either forgets or ignores where he or she is . . . in the most personal of all media.

Why would anyone respond to, or even read, a communication like the one in Figure 11-1, whose opening suggests a benefit so thin and nonspecific that it generates no emotional reaction?

Figure 11-1. Generate emotional reaction.

Subj:	**Tackle tough deadlines with WebEx!**
Date:	4/3/2001 10:56:13 AM Pacific Daylight Time
From:	BillComm.716@Info.dbasenews.com (Webex)
To:	hglewis1@aol.com

Dear Sales & Marketing Executive,

Ease the tension in your fast-paced sales and marketing department—and meet demanding deadlines more effectively than ever. Put our powerful Web conferencing service to work for you!

Regrettably, many of the openings you are about to see are on this list because they're misleading. The assumption that e-mail targets are yokels may be accurate in a small—and shrinking—percentage of cases. But such an assumption damages the image not only of the sender but also of the medium.

Some subject lines and openings are simply too bald or too flat to match the e-mail medium. Every one of these examples was an actual e-mail subject line. The only change is eliminating the initial caps on many of them. Lack of impact is a contagion among e-marketers. Ask yourself: Why are these weak?

- Save on life insurance.

- Get a FREE consultation with one of our financial advisors!

- Low rates

- Home loan alert

- Important message!

- How to measure training success

- Consider refinancing now.

- Online, Refinance Now With Today's Low Rates!

- Great deals at great prices!

- [Online name], Savings Up To 70% On Term Life Protection!

- Business network solutions

- Accessorize your small business!

- If You Qualify As A "Beta-Tester" Your Success Is 100% Guaranteed!

- In the spotlight

- Home improvement 1-2-3

- Planning to buy or sell?

- When your bank says no, we say yes

- Take control of your finances

- Would you be seriously interested in a way to generate income from home?

- RE: Helping you lower your life insurance rates FREE HELP!

- REVEALED: Savings Of Up To 70% On Life Insurance! FREE QUOTE!

- Increase Sales with Mass Faxing! One Million Fax Numbers Only $149.00!

- Special software offer

- Quality is not just a buzzword with us. It's a way of life.

- Is your family protected?

- The power of incentives

- Vive la difference!

- 3M projectors get personal

- NEW animations for employee communications

- Cut corporate travel costs with WebEx.

- 30% cash guarantee

- Use Membership Rewards® points to purchase any product

- Coming soon to your computer screen

- We'll help lower your life insurance rates!

- Tune in to savings!

- Learn to buy & sell like a pro

- Here is your low-cost term life insurance

- Preselected Visa Card! As low as 2.99% Intro APR!

- To know me is to love me

- Debt consolidation.

- We'll refinance your home.

- Get a FREE debt-reduction quote.

- Debt consolidation can be your answer.

- Earn Clickmiles.

- You're eligible to apply.

- Anabolic bodybuilding pharmaceuticals

- All-star savings on rental cars

- Burn CDs, Spark your Creativity

- Interested in bargains?

- Do you owe money?

An easy, logical, and increasingly necessary test when preparing commercial e-mail messages is the self-analysis: If I were reading this instead of sending it, would I be bored? Would I quickly conclude I'd seen and rejected similar wording many times before? Would I just be an unmotivated reader?

If the answer to any of those questions is yes, the solution is simple enough: Write a stronger, more motivational message.

CHAPTER 12

Structuring Sentences and Paragraphs That Persuade

Most e-mail text runs the entire width of the page. The average is sixty-five characters . . . which is a lot.

Note the difference in reading ease between this sentence:

I'm taking a chance on you, because of the source from which your name came to me.

. . . and the following passage:

I'm taking a chance on you.

I'll tell you why.

It's because of the source from which your name came to me.

Reader comfort is a significant e-mail factor. In fact, for first e-mails, it can be *the* most significant factor, carrying even more weight than the offer.

Staccato Bursts and Bulleted Copy

Bulleted copy fits e-mail. But be careful: If the reader senses artifice, the device has backfired. An example of bulleted copy:

I'm taking a chance on you.

I'll tell you why:

- *You're bright.*

- *You're perceptive.*

- *You own the right car.*

I'm serious. You do own the right car.

And that car can be the key to an opportunity I'm going to spell out once.

Compare the bulleted copy with this version, which is almost word for word:

I'm taking a chance on you.

I'll tell you why: You're bright, you're perceptive, and you own the right car.

I'm serious. You do own the right car. And that car can be the key to an opportunity I'm going to spell out once.

The bullets break the message into short bursts, each of which not only prevents boredom but presents an easily digested thought before hitting the targeted individual with the next one.

So if this works, why is there a caution to be careful? Because when the e-mail writer puts thoughts into bulleted copy just because somebody suggested bulleted copy—and not because the presentation matches the technique—the ploy becomes transparent, as in the following example:

> _I personally am convinced that you will be interested in a free copy of my "White Paper" on retirement planning. This is why:_
>
> - _You're a sophisticated investor._
>
> - _That is why I want you to have this "White Paper."_
>
> - _If you like what you read, I can send you an exact Planning Primer, matching your personal finances and goals._
>
> - _Your future is in your hands. Let me help with planning that really can pay off in years to come._

The artificiality of those bullets is obvious. The reader quickly identifies the message as advertising. So much for rapport!

Conversation Is King

If a telemarketing script abandons the principle of mirroring conversational speech, the individual representative can cover, to some extent. Although he or she won't be able to overcome a phrase like "We shall attempt to provide satisfaction," the best bandage over this misguided rhetoric would be heavy emphasis on the word _shall._

Emphasis in e-mail offers the following options:

- Italics

- Boldface

- Italics and boldface

- Underlining

- Color change

- "Produced" (with art or animation) message

- Sound

That these options exist doesn't mean that any of them are effective substitutes for mirroring conversational speech.

TIP

"I" is superior to "We" for establishing a relationship. "We" is superior to "I" for assuming corporate responsibility. Including both within the same message is completely logical, as long as the test clarifies who "I" am and who "We" are.

Generally, relaxed wording that avoids the stiffness and artificiality of formal communication generates greater rapport.

Greater rapport = greater response

Take a Look at This!

Usually, the imperative not only commands attention but also establishes a position of authority. If properly worded, it doesn't annoy. For example: "Take a look at this!"

Take a look at what?

When the sender has an information base about the recipient, a photograph can be a huge asset. A new telephone, a designer garment, an automobile, a prize, an advanced golf club, money—you can enhance whatever excites the reader by using a show-and-tell method.

In other chapters, this book discusses the pros and cons of rich media and illustrations versus straight text. As those other references point out, no rule is absolute, and in e-mail we have an easy and accurate testing medium. A picture might boost response; or, either because the user can't "read" the image . . . or because the representation isn't parallel to desire . . . or because the very insertion of an image reveals the synthetic nature of the message, quickly exposing the commercial intention . . . a picture might suppress response. So we test.

When testing, having the subject line refer to the illustration adds credentials and reduces the risk of instant rejection. That is where the combination of enthusiasm and dynamic verbiage can make a "clickable" difference.

But understand the downside: Having the subject line refer to the illustration destroys the test when testing against plain text, because the reference makes no sense. So the subject line changes for the text version, which again muddies the test.

Parts of Speech

Because the imperative has greater power than the declarative, verbs have greater power than nouns. (See Chapter 7 for an explanation of the relative power of various parts of speech.) Second-person verbs—those implying "you"—have greater power than either first-person (implying "I/We") or third-person (implying "he/she/they") verbs.

Figure 12-1, which has a power-verb opener in the subject line, is more likely to grab and hold attention than a more conventional opening, such as "attention" or the overused "announcing." The imperative verb *hear* demands attention. Visualize the weakness of this e-mail had it opened with, "You can hear every MLB game!" The one negative aspect is that initial capitalization in the subject line reveals that this message is advertising.

Figure 12-1. Hear every MLB game!

Subj:	**Hear Every MLB Game!**
Date:	9:47:20 PM Pacific Daylight Time
From:	news@real-net.net (Sports News)
To:	hglewis1@aol.com

(For e-mailing list removal information see bottom of e-mail.)

Hear Major League Baseball Live in your RealPlayer(R)

From opening day to the pennant races, RealPlayer 8 Plus is the only place online to hear every MLB game live! You can't be a real fan without it!

Click here to get MLB action now:
Click Here

Your Online Box Seat to Major League Baseball
- Join now and get EXCLUSIVE audio broadcasts of every MLB game.
- Follow your favorite team at home or on the road.
- Keep up with your fantasy players live, all season long.

RealPlayer Plus offers a full line-up of features
In addition to MLB, you'll also get:
- Our best player, RealPlayer 8 Plus
- Amazing audio and video with new RealAudio 8
- Full-screen video with RealVideo 8 (requires a P3 processor)
- Easy access to 2500+ radio stations

Get it now:
Click Here

Nouns are next in line. But pronouns, especially the pronoun "it," are pitifully weak as openers.

Because advertising is adjectival—adjectives are the standard grist of advertising—adverbs command more attention than adjectives if only because they are less common.

The Punctuation Factor

Hyperbole is out. No, it isn't our fault. It's the fault of all those hyperbolic marketers who came before us, tossing exclamation points around like so much chaff. The result has been predictable.

TIP

When enthusiasm goes over the top and becomes either shrill or implausible, it then is suspect. Reader enthusiasm diminishes.

That last tip may not have been necessary, because it's true not only in e-mail but in all interpersonal relationships.

Structuring sentences and paragraphs, unlinked to persuasion, is as unprofessional as any e-mail originator can be. The rule is uncomplicated:

Credibility is the key to persuasion. And persuasion is the key to e-mail success.

Neither a bland announcement such as, "We're in business and this is what we have to offer," nor a shrill yelping for attention can match the effectiveness of credibility tied to persuasion. In an era in which the initials CRM (Customer Relationship Management) are such constant buzz-initials—and are so constantly maimed and damaged by dilettantes and linguistic brutes—the serious e-marketer can't ask too often, "Have I been credibly persuasive?"

How to Reduce Opt-Outs

Sweet are the uses of adversity.

When a customer, subscriber, or interested party opts out, is that the end of the affair?

If you think so, you're out of touch with the realities of e-marketing.

The valid assumption is that this person has opted out of getting e-mail from you—not of the relationship with you.

Hard proof exists that these names remain valuable. A major e-marketer tested direct mail—yes, snail mail—to its regular customers and to opt-outs. The test involved hundreds of thousands of names to ensure validity. Note these results:

All segments were profitable except the group that had opted out more than a year before and had not been contacted by any means. The most recent opt-outs had a higher response than any opt-ins other than three-times-plus multibuyers. Curiously, while an enclosed mailing pulled better than a jumbo postcard to opt-outs, this wasn't universally true to the opt-ins, suggesting that a lengthier, more formal communication better helped to restore or maintain the relationship.

Direct mail to opt-outs holds another potential benefit: It always should include an incentive to opt back in, and a substantial percentage will take advantage of this option.

Opting out can be as simple and as pleasant as the message in Figure 13-1. If the e-marketer ignores the request, the next message may include a threat.

Figure 13-1. How to opt out.

Subj:	**get this straight[Fwd: Re: List Subscriber email newsletter - 2 For 1 Inkjet.com]**
Date:	12:02:35 AM Pacific Daylight Time
From:	Jefferson@frii.com (Jefferson Co.-William & Mary Jefferson)
Sender:	mailinglist-request@premiuminkjet.com
To:	sales@2for1inkjet.com, mailinglist@premiuminkjet.com

Please do not send any more messages our way
thanks
————— Original Message —————
Subject: Re: List Subscriber email newsletter - 2 For 1 Inkjet.com
Date: Mon, 2 Apr 2001 23:17:28 EDT
From: RedLocks2@aol.com
To: littleone4l@hotmail.com,

Special Treatment: A Mixed Blessing

The flood of attention to e-marketing has prompted many marketers—in fact, it may be most marketers—to offer unique benefits and perks for an online response.

Synergy seems to apply when a marketer e-mails a customer with news of a forthcoming direct-mail package or printed catalog, and/or highlights from that direct-mail package or catalog. Those who employ this technique say response to both goes up. This inexpensive procedure is certainly worth testing.

Airlines routinely present special discounts not available elsewhere. The argument (and it may be unassailable) is that online reservations are the least expensive to process and also bypass commissions paid to travel agents.

Discounting quite naturally bleeds over to the next and more intimate plateau of the seller/seller relationship—e-mail. Once a visitor becomes a customer, the probability of exercising an opt-out option is greatly reduced. Once the customer becomes a multibuyer, the possibility of opt-out falls to near zero.

Companies such a The Sharper Image say their online offers may be more incentive-laden than the same individual might find in the company's printed catalogs. Omaha Steaks sells its so-called overstocks by e-mail, pointing out that comestibles cannot be stored as hard goods can, and e-mail volume can be tuned to the amount of product on hand.

Vitamin/supplement suppliers regularly e-mail short-term offers for specific vitamins and supplements. Office supply companies e-mail special discount offers with a short expiration date. Retailers e-mail coupons redeemable in their stores, provided the coupons are presented before the expiration date.

The more specific the expiration date, the greater the verisimilitude. So "Good until midnight, Saturday, September 7" has greater impact than "Good through Saturday, September 7."

In each case, the apparent supremacy of e-mail diminishes and denigrates other means of force-communication. Broadcast media, newspapers, and magazines can't match the immediacy; direct mail can't match the timeliness.

A marketer isn't (and shouldn't be) concerned with catering to a specific medium. What matters are the two key elements of competitive survival: growth and profit. So exploiting the uniqueness of e-mail is appropriate.

Keeping Them Happy

The offer of free shipping seems to be the champion among the various incentives e-mail retailers can bring to the marketing arena. How long this will keep its power is questionable, because many e-marketers have adopted free shipping as standard, thereby eliminating it as a private incentive in favor of the overall image it adds to everything the company sells.

In such cases, customer loyalty being a chimera, e-marketers still include free shipping as an incentive in e-mail messages—assuming, quite correctly, that many visitors and customers are unaware of the prevalence of the free-shipping incentive or have forgotten it.

Those who deal in service rather than product constantly look beyond newsletters and sweepstakes as ways to reduce opt-outs. Information can hold fragile loyalty, but only if the information seems to be more useful to the recipient than it is to the sender.

Benefits and Detriments

The ongoing benefits of promoting specials by e-mail are twofold:

1. Recognition that special treatment is ongoing is a huge aid in reducing opt-outs, even among those who haven't responded to a particular offer.

2. Recipients of special e-mail offers are far more likely to be viral mail exponents and to make recommendations than would be the case if the e-mails simply mirrored offers also available elsewhere.

One Downside? Many Downsides?

One downside that has caused much comment is the resentment of those who, through inability or indolence, fail to share in the discounts. Another is the inevitable proletarian connotation of e-mail discounts. A third is the natural child of the second, an "I prefer personal shopping" attitude. A fourth is the fatigue factor stemming from e-mail overpitching (see Chapter 14), which leads not only to reduced response but also to the dreaded opt-outs.

Keeping Them Slathering with Anticipation

Back in what now seems like ancient times, when Coca-Cola was available only in six-ounce bottles, most marketing experts applauded the concept of leaving the consumer wanting just a little more.

The psychology remains absolutely sound: Leave them wanting just a little more.

Invariably, online newsletters with a high opt-out ratio do not do that. They don't lead off with dynamite. They don't carry a provocative story over to the next issue. They don't include a preview of a challenging article in the next issue, or even the date of the next issue.

Newsletters that abide by just a few simple rules cannot only achieve better pass-along ratios but assure themselves of ongoing readership. Three of those rules:

- Include teasers of what will be in the next newsletter.

- Lead with power, not puff.

- Keep articles segmented and short.

The more readable the newsletter, the less likely that opt-outs will occur. Survival in the jungle of e-mailed newsletters demands brightness, useful information, and occasional diversions. The newsletter in Figure 13-2 seems to accomplish all three.

(*text continues on page 204*)

Figure 13-2. Readability helps to lower opt-out rate.

Subj:	**Lawyers not worth trouble they cause**
Date:	8/30/ 4:07:20 AM Eastern Daylight Time
From:	InformationWeek@update.informationweek.com (InformationWeek Daily)
To:	hglewis1@aol.com

GOOD MORNING! Today is Aug. 30, and this is ... InformationWeek Daily! Business innovation powered by technology, brought to you by InformationWeek magazine. Check out informationweek.com

****

This issue sponsored by informationweek.com.
Need information on the hottest IT issues? Check out the new White Paper Library on informationweek.com. You'll find thousands of FREE white papers and case studies that will help you gain the knowledge you need today for the results you need tomorrow. whitepapers.informationweek.com

****

           - TODAY'S HEADLINES -
     ** WORKPLACE: IT Hiring Still Hampered By Salaries
     ** Lucent Outsources Trade-Management Function
     ** Law Prof: Lawyers Threaten Open-Source Movement
     ** Inktomi, BroadVision Integrate Software
     ** TECH STOCKS: Big Dips On Wall Street
     ** The IWeek Trivia-palooza Continues
QUOTE OF THE DAY -
"If they give you ruled paper, write the other way."
- e. e. cummings. Mess with The Man today.

- TOP STORIES -

** WORKPLACE: IT Hiring Still Hampered By Salaries

While rising unemployment has loosened the tight supply of IT workers, companies are still having a hard time coming up with salaries that attract and retain the good ones, according to a study by IT consulting firm Cutter Consortium.

The top three staffing headaches are salary demands, recruiting experienced people, and retaining staff, according to the survey. Forty-seven large and midsized U.S. firms responded. Only 24% of respondents say they pay above-average salaries to attract and retain staff. The most popular inducement was flexible hours, used by 71% of respondents. Chris Pickering, who conducted the study, says tight budgets and strict human-resources policies make it difficult for companies to pay better. "I've told client companies to be more flexible, but invariably they come back and say that human resources doesn't allow us to offer higher salaries," says Pickering.

It's worth noting that the study shows IT staffing ranks a distant fourth among the top concerns facing IT departments; an overwhelming majority ranked aligning IT with business strategy as the top issue, followed by IT budgets and legacy systems. But even though the greater availability of IT workers has companies less concerned about IT staffing than other issues, Pickering thinks now is a good time to get competitive with paychecks. "Companies willing to pay higher salaries will be able to take their pick of applicants," he says. "Once the economy improves, many of those people may not be available." - Mary Hayes

Read on at

Demand For IT Pros To Fall 44%

informationweek.com/story/IWK20010402S0005

Salary Strongholds

informationweek.com/835/salary.htm

** Lucent Outsources Trade-Management Function

In an effort to cut costs, Lucent Technologies Inc. is

(continues)

Figure 13-2. (*continued*)

outsourcing its global-trade-management operations to Vastera
Inc. in a five-year deal. Lucent will pay $25 million for the
first three years of service. Neither company would divulge
details about the last two years of the deal.
Vastera will handle export and import management for Lucent's
U.S. operations. As part of the agreement, Lucent will distribute
Vastera's track-and-trace software, TradeSphere, to all Lucent
divisions.

As the economic slump continues, global companies are starting to
look at their core competencies and figure out ways to cut or
outsource tangential activities, says Mike Bittner, a director
with AMR Research. "All major multinational enterprises have
horror stories about handling global logistics," he says. "They
were forced to tackle it internally because they didn't have an
alternative." Now, with firms like Vastera appearing, Bittner
says more companies will outsource. He adds, "If Lucent does
this, others in the high-tech industry will say 'why aren't we
doing this?' " - Tischelle George

Go deeper. Read
Ryder's Movin' On
informationweek.com/thisweek/story/IWK20010621S0027

Global Logistics Technologies Wins Deal With DuPont
informationweek.com/story/IWK20010212S0005

** Law Prof: Lawyers Threaten Open-Source Movement

SAN FRANCISCO—Stanford Law School professor and cyberspace
expert Lawrence Lessig exhorted software developers Wednesday to
lend their voices and money to defeating intellectual-property
laws that he says chill innovation.

Speaking at the LinuxWorld Conference and Expo here, Lessig said
new regulation on electronic content distribution—and the
changing nature of the Internet—threaten to alter the balance
between free distribution and controlled content. Lessig has
advised the courts on the Microsoft antitrust case, written on
Internet law, and clerked for Supreme Court Justice Antonin
Scalia. "You shouldn't like me—I produce lawyers for a living,"
Lessig said. "You built an extraordinary platform for innovation,
and my kind is working to shut it down."
The Internet's architecture doesn't discriminate by content.
"That system is being changed," he said. Unlike traditional
telcos, cable TV and wireless telcos can favor certain types of
traffic. And U.S. laws, such as the 1998 Digital Millennium
Copyright Act (which makes it illegal to distribute tools that
can be used to circumvent copyrights), give Hollywood "perfect
control" over how its content is distributed, Lessig said.
Ultimately, "certain companies and certain nations are in better
positions to innovate than others."

And open-source advocates aren't helping matters by attacking all
intellectual-property protection with "crude"
oversimplifications, Lessig said. The problem is, he said, too
many find it "more fun to blather on [open-source message board]
Slashdot" instead of actually doing something about the problem.
Entertainment lawyers and big IT companies have "seized the high
ground," he said. "The people who can make a difference in this
battle are you." - Aaron Ricadela

For more background, read
Tales From The Encrypt
informationweek.com/thisweek/story/IWK20010711S0010

Federal Court Hears DVD Case Appeal
informationweek.com/story/IWK20010501S0010

** Inktomi, BroadVision Integrate Software

(continues)

Figure 13-2. (*continued*)

Inktomi Corp., looking to further entrench itself with its growing stable of corporate customers, is allying with BroadVision Inc. in order to integrate its search software with BroadVision's One-To-One Enterprise architecture. The arrangement enables Inktomi customers who also have One-To-One to find content stored in the BroadVision content repository.

Inktomi wants its customers to be able to search everywhere in their networks, rather than having to use search engines in each app. The company is trying to integrate with a variety of software vendors. Inktomi got into the corporate search business last June when it bought Ultraseek Corp. from Go.com, the failed Web portal closed earlier this year by the Walt Disney Co. Paul Karr, Inktomi's director of alliances, says relationships like the one forged with BroadVision are crucial. "There's a need for people to find information wherever it's located, without having to know where it's located," says Karr.

Hadley Reynolds, a Delphi Group analyst, says BroadVision has similar integration arrangements with Verity Inc., but that Inktomi's less-expensive, pared-down engine may have offered BroadVision with sought-after pricing flexibility. Reynolds says search capabilities are crucial to companies that have implemented sophisticated content-management apps, and that companies using BroadVision's One-To-One as the architecture behind their corporate portals benefit from employees being able to use that portal to search for content companywide.
- Tony Kontzer
For related coverage, see
Owens Corning Uses BroadVision Software To Personalize Web Site
informationweek.com/story/IWK20010727S0005

Inktomi Has A Busy Day
informationweek.com/story/IWK20010717S0007

** TECH STOCKS: Big Dips On Wall Street

Wall Street spent its third straight day in the red as the major indexes posted losses. The retreat was fueled in part by news that the second-quarter U.S. gross domestic product posted its worst growth since 1993. The quarter's .7% growth was almost half that of the first quarter.

On top of that, traders had to deal with a spate of earnings warnings. Advanced Micro Devices Inc. warned of falling sales and an operating loss in the third quarter. Shares of the chipmaker sank 4.4%, to $14.20. Telecom-software company Comverse Technology Inc. also warned of a second-quarter earnings shortfall, and fell 8.8%, to $26.05. Juniper Networks Inc. tumbled 7%, to $15.54, after Merrill Lynch trimmed its earnings estimates for the company.

When the closing bell rang, the InformationWeek 100 was down 1.7%, to 304.16, and the Nasdaq Index had shrunk 1.2%, to 1,843.17. Volume on the Nasdaq exchange was moderate at 1.5 billion shares. The Dow was hit just as badly, falling 1.3%, to 10,090.9; an 18-month low. The S&P 500 also slid further south, losing 1.1%, to 1,148.56. - David M. Ewalt

- InformationWeek 100 -
     (informationweek.com/financial)

Company.................$ Close Price...$ Change...% Change

Wednesday's Winners:
MicroStrategy (MSTR).............2.49.......0.09........+3.8%
Interwoven (IWOV).................7.47.......0.27........+3.8%
Vodafone AirTouch (VOD).....19.64......0.54........+2.8%
Palm (PALM)..........................3.68.......0.10........+2.8%
BEA Systems (BEAS)...............16.44......0.38........+2.4%

(continues)

Figure 13-2. (*continued*)

Wednesday's Losers:
VeriSign (VRSN)...............38.69.......-5.95........-13.3%
Comdisco (CDO)...............0.80......-0.10.......-11.1%
BroadVision (BVSN)..........1.82........-0.16.........-8.1%
Ariba (ARBA)....................2.29........-0.20.........-8.0%
Amazon.com (AMZN)......9.19........-0.78........-7.8%

** The IWeek Trivia-palooza Continues

Answer the question below and a second, related question at
informationweek.com/breakaway
and you could win a chic, denim InformationWeek shirt. One winner
will be chosen randomly from correct respondents. But hurry; the
entry deadline is Aug. 31. You'll find a submission form at the
Web site. In mid-November, a grand-prize winner will be drawn
from all correct submissions and awarded another cool prize.
(We're rummaging through the prize closet now.)

This week's question: What sitcom was spun off from "The
Jeffersons"?

The answers to our last question: It was Marlon Brando and Robert
DeNiro who won Oscars for portraying the same character (Vito
Corleone) in the movies "The Godfather" and "The Godfather Part
II." Anthony Torres was the lucky winner. We'll have a new
brainteaser for you Sept. 17.

Daily specials and tips can help e-marketers who want to keep
opt-outs to a minimum. Recognizing that many recipients don't
open e-mail every day, proper marketing psychology suggests
including a submessage such as:

Missed yesterday's special?

You still can get it until midnight tonight.

[Repeat the special]

> Opt-outs may be more of an impulsive decision than opt-ins. Dulling that impulse is nothing other than smart marketing.

TIP

In an e-mail newsletter, when including a preview of a forthcoming revelation, position that preview early in the text. Unusual type treatment may help grab the eye. Leaving this vital component to the end can result in many recipients, bored by apparent sameness, not seeing it at all and concluding that receiving the newsletter isn't worth a continuing effort.

CHAPTER 14

The Interval Enigma: How Often Should You E-Mail?

Asking, "How often should you e-mail?" parallels asking, "How much is a house?"

Frequency usually depends on one of two factors. One is the *frequency differential,* which separates daily wisdom, newsletters, and specials from e-mails whose timeliness isn't as clearly defined. The other is the *eight-level scale,* which determines (climbing up or down the evolutionary scale) where a specific individual might be relative to your organization (or you as an individual).

The eight-level scale is simple enough:

- *First level:* Inquiry

- *Second level:* One click-through

- *Third level:* Second visit

- *Fourth level:* Transaction

- **Fifth level:** Second transaction

- **Sixth level:** Multiple transactions

- **Seventh level:** Advocate

- **Eighth level:** Forwards your communication to others

A Multiplicity of Opinions

As is true of almost every facet of e-mail, everyone associated with this phenomenal medium seems to be an expert. What many experts overlook are the eight-level scale and the frequency differential.

FloNetwork, an e-mail services provider, was quoted in *The Wall Street Journal* with a suggestion that seems sensible—no more than once a week.

Other opinions range from daily to monthly.

Daily works if the recipient expects a daily update. That is the frequency differential in action.

TIP

A daily newsletter will generate opt-outs at a far greater rate than a daily brief news flash.

Climbing the evolutionary scale toward the eighth level increases receptivity of more frequent communications, provided those communications attend to the frequency differential.

Uncontrollable is the number of e-mails from opposing sources. This avalanche becomes increasingly less threatening as the marketer nudges or cajoles a target up the scale.

Some Interesting Experiments

Palm Inc. instituted a procedure for e-mailing tricks and tips for using its handheld devices. The interval between e-mails was based on the estimated time to become familiar with the previous tricks and tips.

Many believe tying interval to event is the most logical answer to the "How often?" question. An event may be the date of a purchase; it may be a personal circumstance such as a birthday or anniversary. It even can be a timed gap between contacts initiated by the customer.

A number of catalogers and retailers have had superior results from using e-mail as a preliminary announcement, then following up the "sneak preview" with an actual offer. Some catalogs and stores report even better luck going directly for the sale, with the sneak preview being an in-advance-of-the-general-public opportunity to buy an item.

TIP

Don't let enthusiasm for the medium lead you to overestimating the reader anticipation a preliminary announcement can generate. Test it against e-mails that include actual offers.

Overwhelming an Online Customer

Can you overwhelm an online customer? The answer lies in the last word of the question: *customer*. The more logically that a marketer can regard a message recipient as a customer, the less likely it is that the recipient will regard frequent messaging as too many.

Most of the auction sites send daily reminders to their frequent bidders. Opt-outs are almost nonexistent, because the bidders regard the auctions as their supplier-partners.

Does that include unsuccessful bidders who haven't connected with many (or any) successful bids? Absolutely. The partnership depends not on actual purchase but on *intent*.

The most common reason for recipients either asking the sender to stop or wishing the sender would stop, without sending that sender a message requesting cessation, is lack of offer or dull-ness of offer.

Vendors become trapped in their own device: "We're sending a daily e-mail to our customers." What is in that e-mail? Like many newsletters, once the golden glow of actually instituting a procedure has begun to dim, supplying content becomes a chore. And bore-dom, regardless of who originates it, is contagious.

So whether the frequency is daily or weekly, an ancient force-communication question should be the driver: If I were getting this instead of sending it, would I find it exciting?

"Exciting" doesn't mean the pulse has to pound. It means what the e-mail says, and how the e-mail says it, should stimulate an emo-tional response.

If you're unable to produce e-mails that consistently generate an emotional response, you're e-mailing too frequently. If you find yourself backed up with unsent offers because you have too many available discounts, prizes, recognitions, or advance news items, you may be e-mailing too infrequently.

TIP

The natural indicator that you're e-mailing too frequently is a surge of opt-outs. But don't necessarily relate the opt-outs to how often you e-mail. More often, the cause is content, not frequency.

Newsletter Frequency

Newsletter frequency ranges from occasional to monthly to weekly to daily. Each has an advantage.

The occasional newsletter may be greeted with enthusiasm if the subject matter is dear to the heart of the recipient. Interval isn't a factor, because most people identify an occasional newsletter as a monthly.

The monthly newsletter should identify itself as a monthly. This adds a patina of importance and helps assure readership of the newsletter (and its accompanying sponsor messages, if any).

The weekly newsletter should arrive at the same time each week. This is a pattern-builder and overcomes the problem of a Monday issue date since the newsletter is dated "Week of . . ." with Monday as the starting date.

The daily newsletter is dangerous unless editing is professional. Too often, the desire to be in constant touch overrides the need to provide fresh information. The result can be stale, poorly written, or irrelevant content. Best success in daily newsletters seems to attend communications from organizations and computer-related senders who carefully choose a timely item as the lead.

QVC, the television shopping network, at press time was sending a daily e-mail describing that day's special as shown on cable television. Because each day the prospect sees a new item under unique circumstances, the daily interval is logical.

If a single statement could cover the enigma of how often a marketer should send e-mails, that statement might be: E-mail as often as you have something to offer that has a prayer of matching the buying psychology of those to whom you e-mail.

Monday and Friday— Poor E-Mail Days?

This will be a short chapter, for good reason: Every business e-mailer and every business e-mail recipient knows the drill without requiring explanation or verification.

When the United States Olympic Committee concluded one of its typical commercial agreements, this one with Xerox Corp., for an e-mail test in July 2001, the committee's associate director of Internet marketing announced that the test drop would be on a Tuesday, followed by a rollout to the opt-in database the following day. He said he had timed the drop for those days "because we find much more success in the middle of the week."

So do most other marketers.

The rationale is obvious: Many people—especially those who use computers at a business office—don't sort through e-mail messages over the weekend. The "Monday pile-up" already has become a known factor.

Friday presents a different problem. People are eager to leave their offices, and the amount of attention they give to e-mail (or any communication they may regard as a distraction) isn't as profound as it might be midweek.

The Hurry-Up Response

A report by *eMarketer* highlighted the difference in response time between e-mail offers and conventional direct-mail offers. The report said that 85 percent of e-mail message response comes within forty-eight hours after the message is sent. Compare that to the ancient direct-mail formula of a 55 percent response by the second Monday after the first response came in, with a total of four to six weeks to reach 85 percent.

Many e-mailers don't want to wait forty-eight hours, so they don't. They tabulate comparable response to tests within twenty-four hours, and sometimes less. Response continues to come in, but the advantage to the marketer is the ability to roll out the winner quickly, before market conditions can change.

TIP

Being able to determine a winning message isn't the only benefit from e-mail's quick response. The marriage of database and technology offers another: Send e-mail when specific targets are most likely to respond. Accucast suggests lunchtime as profitable for sending consumer e-mails, because many people catch up on reading their e-mail while eating snacks at their desks.

If You Decide to E-Mail on Monday (or Have to E-Mail on Monday)

If you're e-mailing on Monday, make a positive point of it by using an acknowledgment and rationale *in addition to* the actual message—such as "Let's start the week off right" or "Your Monday morning pick-me-up." Thus, in keeping with sound marketing principles, you eliminate a potential negative and replace it with a positive.

Timeliness is always a potent rationale, one any e-mail recipient understands and validates. The e-mailer should build timeliness into a beginning-of-the-week message as another step in preventing resentment and quick click-aways. That imperative, obviously, should be spelled out in the subject line.

The other key imperative is the absolute need to avoid a bulk-message look. As disastrous as the bulk look may be to any bulk mailer at midweek, on Monday the negative connotations sharply increase.

If You Decide to E-Mail on Friday (or Have to E-Mail on Friday)

If you're e-mailing on Friday, remember where you are. You're at the end of the workweek, so make a positive point of it: "Let's end the week right" or "Your weekend pick-me-up." That way you've sent an acknowledgment and rationale *in addition to* the message proper. Thus, in keeping with sound marketing principles, you eliminate a potential negative and replace it with a positive.

Of course, a parallel exists between Monday messages and Friday messages. Of the two, Friday messages are easier because the weekend is coming up. So one technique, especially for a complex or lengthy message, is the *early* suggestion: "If you don't have time to absorb this now, why not save it and look it over at your leisure during the weekend?"

Does weekend e-mail work? For students and seniors, the answer is yes. For other groups, test.

Does Day of the Week Really Matter?

Sometimes yes. Sometimes no. Awareness of the day can improve response, and improving response is the right way to keep score. Many people won't see your Monday message on Monday. Many people won't see your Friday message on Friday. Should that change your marketing philosophy? It depends on what your philosophy is.

Are you an e-mail business target? Aren't you, as a business recipient, typically less likely to dedicate time for immediate response on Mondays and Fridays?

The philosophy that can't be bested is described in one word: Test.

TIP

Understand the difference between a generalization and a rule. Generally, Monday and Friday e-mails to business recipients are subject to quick deletion without reading. But that is *generally* and *subject to*. Testing, and only testing, will prove whether or not your specific type of message works as well on Monday and Friday—or even better.

Rich Media and Viral Mail

It's natural and expected that technological advances claim a parallel position with the results of improved communication.

As Samuel Clemens (Mark Twain) wrote at the beginning of *The Prince and the Pauper*: "It may have happened. It may not have happened."

Rich media can rightly claim the mantle of being "the e-mail voice of the future." The animation, sound, and live action of rich media are today's technological wonders.

Some e-marketers claim gigantic leaps in response when the message changes from text or HTML to rich media. Others question the primary attention to medium over message. Still others deny any umbrella claim, pointing out that testing is the only sure method of determining whether—in a specific circumstance—rich media are worth their cost.

Another factor, one becoming less significant as software and operating systems catch up to new types of communications, is the ability of a particular computer to "read" not only rich media but also the more basic HTML. A procedure called "Sniffer" technology tells the sender whether the recipient has HTML capability or not. The sender then can transmit a text message to the non-HTML capable computers.

Smart e-marketers often ask, as part of the original sign-up procedure, whether the recipient's computer is HTML-capable. One minor problem is that some recipients don't know what HTML is and will automatically say yes, thinking their answer gives them greater entitlement. (This problem is diminishing almost daily, as HTML capability becomes universal.)

A large number of suppliers offer rich media technology. At this time, some of the leaders are Dynamics Direct Inc., Beema Inc., Talkway Communications, MindArrow Systems, and Viewpoint. These are just a few representative sources of rich product; it's a fertile and heavily inhabited field.

Some who have tested rich media against text suggest that before focusing on rich media, e-marketers should pay primary attention to getting people to open the e-mail message first. Once opened, they agree, rich media may indeed produce a higher response rate. But the effectiveness of rich media as an opening message is unclear.

TIP

When deciding whether to use rich media or plain text, first test the two against each other. If that is not possible, target and hit to the best of your professional ability. Then refine and massage the message.

Rich media as an adjunct may be more effective than rich media as a primary communication. A number of tests have shown that business-to-business e-mails often produce better response from text than from "produced" messages.

For marketers whose product has visual appeal, rich media would be an obvious choice. Movie studios, for example, report great success, as do television programmers who offer snippets of forthcoming shows and producers of certain types of seminars.

Catalogs, flower vendors, and couponers, on the other hand, report mixed results. For some, rich media have proved to be profitable; for others, using text—either with or without links to the Web site—provides greater ease, speed, and flexibility.

For these reasons, some major marketers proceed cautiously. For example, IBM sent e-mail to 6500 Gold Service customers who had opted in for information about its eServer. The basic message went out as a text file, assuming that some users—even IBM customers—had no HTML capability. A link then led to a server that included both music and a rich media presentation. IBM reported that between 11 percent and 15 percent of recipients clicked through to the rich media presentation. About two-thirds of those continued to fill out an electronic form.

Apparently, Big Blue believes in viral mail, because its software makes possible message-forwarding, which appears to be from the forwarder, not from IBM itself.

The company pointed out that it had no intention of making rich media its standard e-marketing approach, because novelty wears out more quickly than a straightforward presentation.

TIP

Rich media require no more technical capability on the part of the message recipient than the ability to receive text. Don't avoid rich media because you fear the possibility of recipient ignorance of the technology; rather, testing rich media against text should generate a conclusion based on the cost-versus-response ratio.

Video E-Mail

A company named DirectNet promotes video e-mail, which, it claims, generates response rates that are substantially higher than HTML. The company claims the rate to be "at least double."

Obviously, video production costs are substantially higher than other procedures. As technology advances in this and other facets of rich media, dedicated e-marketers have additional—and increasingly complicated—choices. This in turn demands increasingly complicated testing, not only of one technique against the other but also of various techniques relative to the type of offer and target demographics.

Many of the marketers who use video e-mail claim that response can be two to three times higher than HTML, especially when the recipient's name is embedded in the message. Others reject this claim on budget grounds, pointing out that just as HTML costs more than plain text, streaming media and video clips cost more than HTML.

MindArrow Systems claims its video e-mail product produces an average click-through rate of 13.5 percent, compared with 1.5 percent for direct mail, 3.8 percent for rich media banner ads, and 5.4 percent for opt-in e-mails. The numbers are impressive, but caution should be exercised when a comparison doesn't match identical messages to identical targets or when results are not tied to costs. Obviously, this procedure will produce extravagantly superior results when used to promote motion pictures, television programming, travel and leisure, or exotic arts. It might not be superior for hotline offers.

Business-to-Business Marketer "Reservations"

At an Online Marketing International Summit in mid-2001, business-to-business advertisers brought up their reservations about rich media e-mails. They are, the agnostics argued, not only costly and cumbersome but also difficult to send through electronic "firewalls," a common safeguard at business e-mail addresses.

A spokesperson for a provider named Gizmos acknowledged that some businesses are blocking both rich media and streaming videos. But, he added, "Ninety-five percent of the time we can get through firewalls."

Attachments also got short shrift at this summit.

One supplier lauded the pass-along rate and click-through rate of rich media e-mails. Weighing pass-alongs and click-throughs against the additional cost is difficult. As the technology evolves, a better scale of comparison and a better way to keep score will exist: weighing pass-alongs and click-throughs not only against the additional cost but also against the amount of business the additional production generates.

TIP

Test only a segment of the list when sending a message in rich media. This conclusion isn't based only on technology. Testing obviously must relate to effectiveness, since many prior tests to business targets have given the edge to text, both in cost and in response.

Is This the Right Medium?

Rich e-mail exists in three principal forms:

1. An HTML message whose graphics and/or sound are embedded in the basic communication. This is the most fundamental and most commonly used form.

2. Streaming media—graphics, sound, and/or video—stemming from a Web server, appearing when the recipient clicks on the message.

3. An attachment to an e-mail message. The word *attachment* describes the problem—it has to be downloaded first before it can be seen and/or heard.

TIP

Rich media's difference is that they are an *experience*; text is a *message*. Is what you have to say of quick significance or importance? This suggests text. Does it require graphics or sound, as movies or CDs do? This suggests rich media. (Note: The word *media* is a plural.)

A quiet problem of rich media is the need for broadband access in order to download without frustration. Fewer than half of U.S. households that are online have high-speed broadband connections, wired or wireless direct linkage to the Internet that avoids the slowness and congestion of telephone modem lines.

Another problem is cost, which easily can reach $10,000. At this time, a typical estimate for production of a thirty-second campaign is $18,000.

So why use rich media, with the limitations, costs, and need for hyperprofessional technical aid? The answer must be increased response from targets to justify the cost. A study showed that rich media command a better than 20 percent higher recall rate—and although recall is meaningless in e-mail—the study indicated a 35 percent higher click-through rate.

TIP

A click-through rate in no way parallels a response rate, any more than opening a direct-mail envelope is parallel to sending an order.

One successful e-marketer made this observation about rich media:

Text [versus] richer and richer messages? I'll buy into richer messages for image development. But then, if I want image development, I want an image they don't have to click to see . . . like a billboard at the exit of a crowded ramp on the expressway. Unless it's cost-justified after the dropout of the no-clickers, you're guessing. Trouble is, with image advertising, you never really know.

I hope everyone decides to use e-mail to augment image development with elaborate technologies that stay ahead of the curve. I hope the rest of them try to build personalization in that medium. In the meantime, my e-mail is going to be used as a direct response vehicle that relies on a compelling message. The skill employed in developing that message, and now, more than ever, the subject line alone, is what will generate response for me.

Another marketer takes an opposing view:

Remember the old rule of direct mail? "A.I.D.A.—Attention, Interest, Desire, Action." If you don't grab attention, the other three don't even exist.

E-mail has become so pervasive you have to shake them up to get even a teacup of attention. Text simply doesn't have the bullets to shake them up.

If ever two opposing viewpoints proved the value of testing, these two do.

Flash-Bashing—One Nasty Opinion

"Flash" is a proprietary display system available from Macromedia, Inc. Flash is heavily used by Web marketers, such as gm.com, and it currently may be the most popular base for corporate "splash screens"—images that pop up to occupy space while a site-page is loading. As such, it is subject to attacks and is sometimes accused of being an overused technology.

An irreverent Web site called Dack.com editorializes:

Macromedia says Flash is "[T]he solution for producing and delivering high-impact Web sites." It's also a solution for making your site highly annoying and downright unusable. Here's why:

Flash has contributed to the amount of gratuitous animation on the Web, and unlike animated GIFs, Flash animations do not respond to your browser's Stop button or your keyboard's Esc key, so they cannot be easily turned off. Users must resort to either covering the offending animation with their hand, or, more likely, leave the site altogether.

By sporting significantly smaller file sizes than equivalent GIF animations, Flash has brought back the splash screen, one of the most irritating of all Web "experiences." Web users typically are looking for content, and presenting them with a content-free splash screen is a sure way to annoy, and give visitors a (good) reason to punt the site.

Incorporating Flash into an HTML page or splash screen is bad, but entire sites built with Flash are positively evil because they make the Web much less usable. Flash sites render useless the browser's Back button and Address bar, and make book-marking pages inside a Flash site impossible. Printing Flash pages from your browser doesn't work, nor does intra-page keyword searching. Finally, Flash sites eliminate HTML links' visited and unvisited colors, and that color-changing feature is the Web's single most important navigational cue.

Dack.com claims to have sponsored a Flash versus HTML test, whose results, scored on a scale from 1 to 5, showed for "Ease of finding specific information": HTML 3.75, Flash 2.5; and for "Overall ease of use": HTML 4.25, Flash 2.5.

(Note: This critique, from Dack.com's Web site, refers more to other Web sites than to e-mail and is printed here without commenting pro or con.)

The Power of Viral Mail

Viral mail—the e-mail incarnation of the venerable member-get-a-member promotions—has been proclaimed an e-mail moneymaker by its users.

For example, it's difficult to believe the results of an e-mailing by Subaru. The automaker claims that an e-mail sent to 100,000 prospects sent in 2001, which touted the 2002 Impreza WRX automobile, brought a 165 percent response—that is, 165,000 click-throughs.

Subaru attributes what seems to be a mild impossibility to viral mail. A box at the bottom of the e-mail invited recipients to enter a friend's address. Subaru then sent the e-mailing to the friend. What makes this even more remarkable is that the e-mail went to rented lists, whose common denominator was "auto enthusiast with active lifestyle."

Planned Parenthood Federation of America e-mailed a viral marketing campaign to 45,000 donors on Independence Day, 2001, which resulted in 3,100 new e-mail members. The message discussed the issue of contraception, included a suggested petition to be delivered to the President of the United States, and suggested that recipients forward the e-mail to friends. According to the organization, a by-product was a group of monetary donations from both new and existing members.

A "catalog of catalogs," Catalog City uses what it calls eGift technology, a form of viral mail. Consumers can send e-mail to family, friends, and business associates, offering a choice of gifts (in different colors and sizes) from one of the Catalog City catalogs. (The procedure works well when trying to find a gift for grandchildren, who may already have or not want toys that otherwise might be sent.)

TIP

Some of Catalog City's marketers declare that viral marketing is a major component of their total business. The tell-a-friend option has an energy few commercial messages can match.

Most experts seem to agree that technology-driven viral marketing is considerably less effective than relationship-driven viral marketing. Including a place or procedure for a personal note validates the forwarded message.

Online referrals are significantly easier to make than mailed or telephoned referrals because the forwarding mechanism often is as easy as typing the name and clicking the mouse.

This subject line is a typical invitation to send viral mail:

AIM's Who's News! Vol. 5 No. 25—Send it to your friends!

Whether that invitation succeeds or not depends on the next sentence. Note the first sentence in Figure 16-1, which may be a clever psychological ploy designed to induce pass-along.

Figure 16-1. A psychological ploy.

Subj:	**Reminder: Required Preventing Workplace Harassment**
Date:	8/31 3:17:49 AM Eastern Daylight Time
From:	courses@learningaction.com
To:	hglewis1@aol.com

PLEASE DO NOT FORWARD THIS MESSAGE, OR IT WILL NOT WORK PROPERLY.
Hello,

You are receiving this message as a reminder that you have requested
to see one of LearningAction's web-based training courses. Starting
the course is easy: Just click on the web link below, or copy it and
paste it into your web browser:

http://www.la2.net/base3.jsp?c=21367&f=f35x98&a=301&b=359&e=310

When you take this course, you will notice that we use state-of-the art technology and real-time audio to enhance your viewing experience. If your computer is enabled for animation, you will automatically receive an animated version of this course. If not, you will receive a non-animated version of the course automatically. Either way, you will not need to download plug-ins or change your configuration in any way.

The e-mail message in Figure 16-2 uses a different tactic. It suggests a pass-along and includes a caution to reinforce the so-called exclusivity factor: "Feel free to forward this, but please don't cut it." Both sender and recipient should consider: Is it too long to be effective?

Figure 16-2. Can shorter be more effective?

Subj:	**Gator.com Goes to Court, A Look at the New Netscape, The New Windows XP, and more**
Date:	8/30/ 10:39:55 AM Eastern Daylight Time
From:	listsupport@internet.com (NewMedia Insider Report)
Reply-to:	listsupport@internet.com (NewMedia)
To:	hglewis1@aol.com

internet.com's
NewMedia Insider Report - What's Next on the Net

Thursday, August 30

:::Feel free to forward this, but please don't cut it:::
:::Sign up for this newsletter at http://www.newmedia.com:::

****
This Week - from Bob Woods, NewMedia Managing Editor

(*continues*)

Figure 16-2. (*continued*)

For our weekly NewMedia review, we take a look at some cool tools one company has come up with for your Palm, PocketPC or whatever flavor of PDA you use. We also examine a legal dust-up that's starting between Gator.com and the Interactive Advertising Bureau over Gator's advertising methods. Gator says it is doing no wrong; the IAB claims Gator's business practices mislead Web site visitors. All of that and much more in Business.

In Design/Development, we start a 2-part series on the new version of Netscape Communicator — the new suite just may surprise you. Also, we examine a way to stream across multiple platforms and file formats at the same time, and we evaluate a new drawing program that's "like a fine wine, in that it gets better with age."

And in Technology, is Microsoft's new Windows XP sending nearly everyone buzzing? The answer is yes, but that group includes lawmakers in Washington. Also, we help you to answer the question you may not want to think about: Do I need tech-liability coverage? Just the thing to consider going into a holiday period, I know...

Here's hoping that you have a great three-day weekend. I'll be at the beach. And now, What's Next on the Net...

****

/————————————————————————-\

JOB SECURITY — CAREER GROWTH — CHALLENGING POSITIONS
The internet.com Careers Channel is powered by dice.com,
the leading online Information Technology (IT) job board.
Whether you need to start your new job today, are
searching for your dream job, or are just wondering what
your skills are worth, you'll find the tools you need to land
your next great job. Don't wait any longer!
http://www.internet.com/sections/careers.html

\————————————————————————adv.-/

THIS WEEK'S NEWS

* BUSINESS
Gator.com Sues the IAB
Round one begins in a legal fight that could have repercussions throughout the Web publishing industry. Claiming that it's had enough of the Interactive Advertising Bureau's "unfounded accusations and threats," Redwood City, Calif.-based Gator is suing the New York-based industry association and seeking to clear its name.
http://www.newmedia.com/default.asp?articleID=3041

Some ttools for Your PDA (A NewMedia REVIEW)
No, the "ttools" above isn't a typo. It's the name of a company that makes some cool tools for PDAs, including combo pens/styli and a security screen that sticks to the top of the device's LCD display.
http://www.newmedia.com/default.asp?articleID=3016

The Power of Passionate Pages
Over a third of all Internet subscribers have stopped surfing because they say the Web offers them nothing they need or want. That may be because content on the Web lacks enthusiasm. Learn how to make your Web site a passionate one.
http://www.newmedia.com/default.asp?articleID=3013

Move to Broadband Changes How the Web is Surfed
The number of residential Internet users with high-speed connections keep rising, signaling not only a change in how consumers access the Internet, but also how they use it once they're online.
http://www.newmedia.com/default.asp?articleID=3003
Search Engines Fail to Draw Marketing Dollars
Search engines may be the top method for finding sites on the Web, but only a small percentage of businesses have dedicated a portion of their marketing budget for building cohesive search engine strategies, according to a new report.
http://www.newmedia.com/default.asp?articleID=3007

(continues)

Figure 16-2. (*continued*)

Flooz to File Bankruptcy
Unable to secure a merger partner and burned by what it described as "dramatic changes in capital markets," alternative currency play Flooz.com has shut down and plans to file for federal bankruptcy protection by the end of this week.
http://www.newmedia.com/default.asp?articleID=3032

Trilegiant Picks Up AOL Marketing Where Cendant Left Off
America Online will continue its discount club program through a deal with Norwalk, Conn.-based membership services giant Trilegiant.
http://www.newmedia.com/default.asp?articleID=3020

Internet Politics Insider
Get the scoop on Internet-related politics, right here. From the Association for Interactive Media (www.interactivehq.org).
http://www.newmedia.com/default.asp?articleID=3012

* DESIGN/DEVELOPMENT
Review: Netscape 6.1 (Part I)
If you've not taken a peek at Netscape for a while, you may be surprised at the new look and feel associated with Netscape 6.1. We have Part I of a two-part review of the new version of the Internet tool.
http://www.newmedia.com/default.asp?articleID=3017

PBS Pushing Multimedia Envelope
While plenty of broadcast outlets are keen on using the Web to help promote their TV programming, PBS and its Web production team are increasingly pushing the medium to show its potential.
http://www.newmedia.com/default.asp?articleID=3042
DevX Launches Largest Free Code Library On The Web
A deal with Sourcebank adds some 27,000 free code samples for C++ and Web scripting languages, such as Perl and JavaScript.
http://www.newmedia.com/default.asp?articleID=3038

Transcoding with Telestream
If you've been looking for a way to stream at the same time across multiple

platforms and file formats, then have a look at Telestream, a company that simplifies streaming media production or transfer of high quality media over the Internet.
http://www.newmedia.com/default.asp?articleID=3009

Review: Canvas 8
Deneba's Canvas software is like a fine wine in that it gets better with age. Unlike wine, the latest version is reusable, won't leave you tipsy, and the only way you wake up looking at something ugly is if you create it that way before you go to sleep.
http://www.newmedia.com/default.asp?articleID=3004

New: Activedit 2.5
The new program lets developers easily enable end-users with quick and easy Web publishing & content management capabilities. It's a Word-type processor embedded into a Web page. Now available in ASP, JSP, and CF flavors.
http://www.newmedia.com/default.asp?articleID=3010

DivXNetworks Releases MPEG-4 Video Codec
After the new format was beta tested in mid-July, DivX says version 4.0 is now virtually bug-free and ready for consumer usage.
http://www.newmedia.com/default.asp?articleID=3014

BurlyBear to Produce Content for TBS
With the potential to reach about 83.3 million households served by TBS Superstation, the deal is a big leap forward for the six-year-old BurlyBear network, which produces edgy, broadband content for college audiences.
http://www.newmedia.com/default.asp?articleID=3021

* TECHNOLOGY
Industry Heralds Delivery of Windows XP to OEMs
Microsoft's newest operating system has the industry buzzing with anticipation.
http://www.newmedia.com/default.asp?articleID=3019

Do You Need Tech Liability Coverage?
Companies that have to deal with all kinds of insurance plans may snicker at

(continues)

Figure 16-2. (*continued*)

tech liability coverage. But many traditional general liability policies don't address technology risks, so tech liability insurance is something to consider.
http://www.newmedia.com/default.asp?articleID=3005

Case Study: Tangram Ensures Prudential's IT Assets
Prudential had little clue about keeping track of its computers and IT systems until it had to gear up for the Y2K crisis. Now, more than two years later, the company is still benefiting from the asset-management software it purchased, in ways it never expected.
http://www.newmedia.com/default.asp?articleID=3008

Turbolinux Updates Supercomputer Clustering Option
Turbolinux has unveiled version 7 of EnFuzion, a clustering technology designed to transform an enterprise's network of Linux, Unix, and Windows servers or workstations into a supercomputer by transparently integrating it into a single operating environment.
http://www.newmedia.com/default.asp?articleID=3018

Excessive Spending on App Servers - Study
Gartner estimates that enterprises have overspent about $1 billion on application server technology solutions since 1998. The report further projects an additional $2 billion may be wasted between now and 2003.
http://www.newmedia.com/default.asp?articleID=3011

Sun Shares Dip After Goldman Sachs Report
Investors react to a Goldman Sachs report that claims Sun may not be out of the dark yet; while long-term prognosis is bullish, GS reserves caution about the hardware firm in the short term.
http://www.newmedia.com/default.asp?articleID=3040

HP Throws Its Arms Around Linux
Palo Alto, Calif.-based computer and printer maker gears up to release high-security version of open source operating system for servers as well as smaller devices.

http://www.newmedia.com/default.asp?articleID=3030

Intel Revs its Engines with 2GHz Chip
Intent on putting some distance between itself and rival AMD, Intel goes
live with Pentium 4.
http://www.newmedia.com/default.asp?articleID=3031

Tiny Technology With a Huge Impact on Mobility
MEMS, a technology which produces micron-sized devices, is poised to have an
enormous impact mobile systems, and therefore on M-Commerce. What is MEMS
and where is it being used?
http://www.newmedia.com/default.asp?articleID=3015

MORE NEWS (From the internet.com Network)

Making Sense of Branding
We discuss the finer points of branding and direct response advertising, and
how to know which type is right for your business.
http://ecommerce.internet.com/news/insights/ebiz/article/0,,10379_873381,00.
html

When Bad Publicity Happens to Good Companies
Even if you run an ethical and honest business, an unsavory alliance can
quickly pull you into the mire. In the "know-all, see-all, report-all"
digital age, not only can a simple transgression ruin your professional
reputation, so could just the mere appearance of impropriety.
http://ecommerce.internet.com/news/insights/ectips/article/0,,10380_872711,0
0.html

The Future of E-Procurement? We'll Wait and See
Electronic procurement seems like a good idea, but it isn't being used for
large, direct purchases. And in addition to previously existing concerns
about security, integration and standards, we can now add a questionable
economy.
http://cyberatlas.com/markets/b2b/article/0,,10091_873291,00.html
This Week's Agenda: Shakedown Street

(continues)

Figure 16-2. (*continued*)

"Shakedown Street" was a vision of urban decay and the kindness that lay underneath. That's a good analog for today's Web. Everything seems to be going to pot and shakedowns are in vogue, but some good things are happening out there too.
http://www.clickz.com/ebiz/ebiz_report/article.php/872601

Advanced Form Presentation & Printing
This three-part article details the dynamic creation of PDF forms with ASP and describes the handling of all the most common form elements. Connect PDF forms to a database and retain, even extend Adobe's portability and printability.
http://www.15seconds.com/issue/010822.htm

Scripting for 5th Generation Browsers and Beyond: Pt. II
Dynamically position your page objects the DOM way! Having covered the nuts and bolts, we now conclude our introduction to DOM based scripting with a practical example.
http://www.webreference.com/programming/javascript/domscripting/2/

JavaScript: Quiz
Here's a simple quiz script that gives the reasoning for each answering.
http://miscellaneous.javascriptsource.com/javascript-quiz.html

Java: SearchToHTML
The SearchToHTML applet performs a simple text search of the files you specify in its parameters. It writes out the results of your searches as HTML in a separate frame or a new window.
http://javaboutique.internet.com/SearchToHTML/
How To Make In-House IT Compete
In-house IT shops are often perceived as less competitive than outsourcers. In response, many CIOs have launched initiatives to "think like a business" when running internal IT organizations. But what exactly does this mean? A management consultant suggests starting by thinking of users as customers.
http://itmanagement.earthweb.com/cio/article/0,,11967_872431,00.html
Sun Ups Performance for Netra X1

Sun ups the performance specs for the Netra X1, its entry-level,
single-processor, rack-optimized server, while leaving the $995 price tag
intact.
http://www.internetnews.com/prod-
news/article/0,2171,9_873521,00.html

When 'Pay As You Go' Storage Service Pays Off
The Storage Service Provider market may be getting its share of bumps
and
bruises, but the pay-as-you-go model is a good match for some enterprises.
http://www.internetnews.com/asp-news/arti-
cle/0,2171,3411_873461,00.html

****

Submit an article to NewMedia:
http://www.newmedia.com/default.asp?articleID=2677
****

NewMedia is now reviewing products/services. For details:
http://www.newmedia.com/default.asp?articleID=2678
****

Contact Us!
Questions? Comments? Please e-mail them to NewMedia Managing Editor Bob
Woods (bwoods@internet.com). Please do not send unsubscribe requests
to this
address—instructions for that appear at the very bottom of this newsletter.
You can also subscribe directly from our Web site, at
http://www.newmedia.com.

newmedia-insider-report-text Is Powered By http://By.SparkLIST.com/
In-house vs. Outsourced Email List Hosting: Are you
paying too much for your email list management? Download
the FREE REPORT: http://SparkLIST.com/free-report/
~~~~~~

(continues)

Figure 16-2. (*continued*)

Advertising: If you are interested in advertising in our newsletters, call
Ian Flynn on 1-203-662-2876 or send email to mailto:nsladsales@internet.com

~~~~~~

For contact information on sales offices worldwide visit
http://www.internet.com/mediakit/salescontacts.html

~~~~~~

For details on becoming a Commerce Partner, contact David Arganbright
on 1-203-662-2858 or mailto:commerce-licensing@internet.com

~~~~~~

To learn about other free newsletters offered by internet.com or
to change your subscription visit http://e-newsletters.internet.com

~~~~~~

internet.com's network of more than 160 Web sites are organized into 16
channels:

Internet Technology	http://internet.com/it
E-Commerce/Marketing	http://internet.com/marketing
Web Developer	http://internet.com/webdev
Windows Internet Technology	http://internet.com/win
Linux/Open Source	http://internet.com/linux
Internet Resources	http://internet.com/resources
ISP Resources	http://internet.com/isp
Internet Lists	http://internet.com/lists
Download	http://internet.com/downloads
International	http://internet.com/international
Internet News	http://internet.com/news
Internet Investing	http://internet.com/stocks
ASP Resources	http://internet.com/asp
Wireless Internet	http://internet.com/wireless
Career Resources	http://internet.com/careers
EarthWeb	http://www.earthweb.com

~~~~~~

To find an answer - http://search.internet.com

~~~~~~

Looking for a job? Filling an opening? - http://jobs.internet.com

R.I.P.: Radical Mail

Radical Mail was a rich media approach by Radical Communication of Marina del Rey, California, a technology the now-defunct company used to make e-mail similar to an actual Web site, by using video and sound.

The technology had promise. MGM Consumer Products sent 60,000 Radical Mail e-mails to girls age 13 to 17, selling teen intimate apparel. The content of the mail had recipients clicking to see a Pink Panther video clip. Payoff was a coupon/voucher to be presented to retail stores, thereby tying retail outlets to the e-mail. At the stores, the coupons earned a gift for girls who tried on Pink Panther Intimates.

Actually, the program qualified as a completely integrated campaign, because MGM not only mailed 100,000 postcards but also added a viral mail hook by enabling viewers to send the gift coupon/voucher to three friends each.

In another test, Radical Communication designed a rich media subscription campaign for the publication *The Economist*. Components included a streaming version of the magazine's sixty-second television spot plus heavy use of graphics and photographs. Included was a viral mail component, suggesting the recipient forward the offer to a friend or colleague. (Simultaneously, the magazine sent a parallel subscription offer to nearly 2 million names.) Because results were not disclosed, the effectiveness of this multimedia campaign is difficult to evaluate.

But the demise of this pioneer rich media organization in mid-2001 brought two questions into focus:

1. How could a technique so many had hailed as the future of Internet communications disintegrate so quickly?

2. Does the closing of Radical Mail underscore the difference between novelty and genuine force-communication?

The answer to the first question may be locked in corporate lore. The answer to the second is—in this author's opinion—yes. Novelty entertains; force-communication motivates. The ultimate effectiveness test of any message lies in response.

So the lesson of Radical Mail may be that novelty must weld itself to information or be judged by history as what it is: novelty.

The Ongoing Study: Rich Media vs. Text

Response rates seem to vary so widely that testing on a case-by-case basis is the obvious solution.

SkyGo, a wireless technology and media consulting company headquartered in Redwood City, California, claimed in mid-2001 that a text-only campaign brought a huge response—a 50 percent recall rate, with 3 percent of those who viewed the text e-mail actually buying the product.

ESPN, Ford, and Net2Phone have also reported significant success with text-only e-mails.

By tying text and rich media together, a company named AvantGo, San Mateo, California, claimed that click-through rates for its text advertisements for digital assistants, which linked to a page rich with graphics, were five times higher than other advertisements on the Web.

As cell phones and wireless handheld microcomputers proliferate, arguments for and against both text and rich media can become heated. Proponents of text point out the limited space of Palm units and cell phones; proponents of rich media point out the need to grab and hold attention. In anticipation of greater use of rich media, the 3G wireless systems—relatively new voice and data standards—can raise data transmission speed from the second-generation level of 28 kilobytes to 50 kilobytes per second to a third-generation speed of 100 kilobytes per second.

And that brings us to the ultimate tip: Test. And when you encounter your next marketing project, test again.

17

Sample E-Mails: The Good, the Bad, and the Ugly

Creating an e-mail message that includes both originality and sales expertise is becoming increasingly difficult, since the so-called standard techniques are becoming more and more common.

Our targets may become so immune to frenzy that they no longer respond to it. They certainly will click out of tedious and dull messages. And in a highly sophisticated database ambience, failure to recognize characteristics that help to establish rapport with your target is criminal.

Included in this chapter are examples of e-mail that represent, in the author's opinion, strong and weak messages. Your own computer screen, today, will provide more examples as you're online.

The e-mail message in Figure 17-1 has good text, excellent rapport, and a strong one-to-one approach.

(*text continues on page 244*)

Figure 17-1. Creating a strong one-to-one approach.

Subj:	**$5000 Diet Challenge!**
Date:	9:45:09 AM Pacific Standard Time
From:	seye45y@mail3.blackjackhit.com
Reply-to:	iomnfnend233d@yahoo.com
To:	hjdrth@aol.com
CC:	omeo@aol.com, chgotopson@aol.com, asmoose64168@aol.com, omeob@aol.com, hglewis1@aol.com, asmoose64@aol.com, dtnchgd@aol.com, martex@aol.com, chgotown@aol.com

Hi! My name is Betty Wilson. I got your e-mail address off a post. Please forgive me if I made an error; I'm a two-fingered typist. I put this little note together to show people that it's not impossible to lose any amount of weight that you want! I hope you find this information useful.

I'm married, with 2 boys, ages 14 and 12.

I was getting bigger every year. My weight had hit 264 pounds at age 38. For my height and build, I should have weighed about 175 pounds. That was 89 pounds overweight, clinically obese. My parents were concerned that I was overweight, and growing larger. Every time I lost weight, I gained even more back.

THEN CAME THE CHALLENGE. They said that if I lost weight and got down to my proper weight, they would give me $5,000.

I wanted that money, but even more I wanted to look better and be healthy. I dieted on and off for 7 months, but got nowhere. I was depressed and disappointed.

The $5,000 wasn't as important anymore, although I certainly wanted it. It was more the overall challenge of overcoming what had become about the hardest thing I ever had to do. I suddenly realized just how difficult this weight problem had really become.

I had researched and tried many weight loss programs during my yo-yo dieting years. I did Slim Fast, Cyber vision, soup diets, starvation, "exercise-and-eat-no-fat," chromium picolinate, metabolic enhancers, and more. You name it and I tried it. I lost some pounds with every diet, and then eventually gained it back, usually with a few extra pounds.

I almost gave up. Then, I remembered something I heard about from a friend of mine. He was using a product (some kind of special "Asian berry") his doctor rec-ommended, that helped him lose a lot of weight, FAST. It had been kept a secret for years, until now. An American company hooked up with an Asian scientist and brought the secret here.

Hoping it might help curb my eating problem, I called him up to see how the "berry" stuff (called BERRY TRIM PLUS) was working. He said it was working "GREAT" for him, as well as for other people using it. It contains BRINDALL BERRIES, and other key nutrients, which the Asian scientists found in very rare plants and herbs.

It sounded too good to be true, but I tried everything else. So one more time............. I took Berry Trim Plus every morning; it seemed to help me "wake up" in the morning. I was hitting the snooze alarm less. I had more energy during the day, and slept better at night.

I really noticed a difference. The more I took it, the better I felt. I was staying up later, but was more refreshed in the morning. This was a very different experience compared to other diets; this was a very positive thing.

What a feeling of accomplishment!

Yes, folks, you can still eat, and even eat good stuff. If I had to eat just a salad with no dressing for a meal, I'd GO CRAZY!

My husband, Sal, is shocked! IN 5 MONTHS I LOST 81 POUNDS, AND IT'S STAY-ING OFF! (13 months so far.) I got down to 173 pounds.

It was easy. Anyone can do it. Oh, and yes, I did collect the $5,000. We met my parents for a vacation. They were shocked and delighted; they didn't recognize

(*continues*)

Figure 17-1. (*continued*)

me, even when I stood right next to them. My mom and dad were glad to give me the money. Dad said it was the best investment he ever made and my mom, well, it took a few days for her to pick her jaw up off the floor.

The best reward wasn't the money. It was the reward of being healthy, and looking great again. I have changed, I will never be overweight again. Berry Trim Plus works incredibly.

Well, now I'm the same weight I was in college, wearing denim cutoffs again. I fit in all my 20 year old clothes that I saved hoping I would fit in them again. I still can't believe it happened.
OK, so here comes the big sales pitch, right? Look, if you want to try this product, your life will change after you lose the weight. Believe me, this is the only thing in all the years that worked for me. With all the marketing scams out there, we have to be skeptical. This is not a scam. It really works!

Whether you need to take off five pounds or two hundred, this will help you do it, fast and easy. The company has a money-back guarantee, and they get practically no returns. That says it all, if you ask me. Click on the link below and read other Berry Trim Plus testimonials to check it out. I can assure you that I would not put my credibility on the line unless everything I have told you here were 100% true.

CLICK HERE
God Bless!!

Betty Wilson
This message has been sent to you by an independent Berry Trim Plus affiliate.

The message in Figure 17-2 is too long for this medium. Although the e-mail claims there is nothing to buy, it later asks for $29.95. This sales tactic is an ancient ploy, now resuscitated online.

(*text continues on page 252*)

Figure 17-2. Resuscitating an ancient sales ploy online.

Subj:	**Homeworkers Needed (ia722)**
Date:	11:15:19 PM Pacific Daylight Time
From:	linda9@prodigy.net
To:	UndisclosedRecipients

How to Get Paid at Home
And Make up to $938 Every Week Like Me

Dear Friend,

If you want to make hundreds of dollars a week working right at home, I've got great news. Not only is it possible, but my special methods can make it surprisingly easy.

Hi. I'm Linda Applebee. I've been doing this kind of work at home for over ten years- it's not very complicated. Mainly I insert sales literature into envelopes, seal them, and mail them. It's called "stuffing envelopes" for short. It's a wonderful way to make money. I really enjoy it.

More people would be doing it if they had the facts on how it's done and who actually pays people for it. That's where I can help. I'll tell you the exact methods I use to make money quickly and easily. You can follow my simple instructions and get paid just like me.

My neighbor, Teresa, gave me the idea of sharing this information with others. A few months ago she told me how she had sent payments to several different companies who advertised that they needed envelope stuffers. All she received were useless plans and schemes.

It's too bad she didn't ask me first. I told her the real facts about stuffing envelopes, and I gave her information on a local company that had paid me before. She was eager to check it out.
Nothing To Buy. Immediate Payment.

(continues)

Figure 17-2. (*continued*)

She told me about it the next time I saw her. The company did not charge her any fee or require her to buy anything to get started. They furnished all envelopes, sales letters, mailing labels, and postage stamps free. Teresa stuffed and sealed the envelopes, applied the address labels and postage stamps, and mailed them. When she was done, they immediately paid her based on the number of envelopes stuffed.

Teresa really appreciated the information I gave her. She suggested that I write a book on envelope stuffing so other people who want to make money at home can avoid the trouble she went through. I liked that idea. I enjoy helping others when I can. So I went ahead and wrote the book. That's why I'm sending you this email today.

Secrets That Make It Easy

My book is named "Secrets of Stuffing Envelopes." In it I show you the secrets I use to earn up to $938 a week working part time as an independent contractor. That means I get to do things my way. I work at home when I want and at my own speed. I use whatever methods or shortcuts I like. Companies pay me based on what I produce, and they do not take any deductions from my checks.

My book tells you how you can do the same thing. You can live anywhere in the country, work only when you want, and make more money than people who have regular jobs. And you can keep your business private so even your neighbors won't know about it unless you tell them.

It takes more than just knowing how to insert things into envelopes. The term "stuffing envelopes" refers to several mail marketing activities that are covered in my book. I'll tell you the easy and effective methods that I use. When you do it my way, you do not need any permit or license. You do not have to receive orders. The checks you receive are from the companies that pay you.

Even if you've never done anything like this before, my book makes everything clear- starting with the basics. I explain how to correctly fold and insert letters into envelopes. I caution you about common mistakes to avoid. I explain how to spot misleading envelope stuffing offers and how to connect with businesses that supply everything free and pay for each envelope you stuff.

Everything you need to know is explained in a simple, concise way. You can probabaly read the essential parts and be ready to start in less than an hour. Your first paycheck could be in your hands in as little as ten days.

One Dollar For Each Envelope You Stuff

Many companies advertise that you can make one dollar for each envelope you stuff. Some promise even more. But don't take their word for it. Especially when you have to send them money first just to find out how their program works.
They usually don't tell everything that is involved, such as placing classfied ads. Many of them simply lie altogether. And they will not refund your money.

My book explains how real dollar-per-envelope programs work and how you can take advantage of them. There's no need to pay any money to get into a good one. I'll tell you how.

When I say I make money stuffing envelopes, I am NOT talking about selling my book. I am talking about how other companies pay me the same way you can get paid! You do not have to write any books or sales letters. You do not have to receive any orders. Just follow the directions in my book.

The best envelope stuffing opportunities have no limit on earnings, and they pay based on sales generated. I make a wonderful income this way, working just a few hours a day. But it wasn't always this easy. At first I found myself stuffing an awful lot of envelopes for not very much money. I was happy enough just to be making money at home. Then an exciting discovery changed everything.

Much Higher Income With Less Work

(continues)

Figure 17-2. (*continued*)

About four years ago I happened to meet a unique person who took envelope stuffing very seriously. He had put a lot of thought and effort towards his goal of making as much money as possible with available mailing programs. When he showed me his latest check, I had to catch my breath. It was for over seven thousand dollars! And that's just for one week. It was more that 25 times the size of my check in the same mailing program. Besides that, other companies were sending him checks too!

I had no idea so much money could be made this way. It helped him buy a fabulous home overlooking the ocean. Yet he works just a few hours a day, right there at home. I sure wanted to know how he did it. Fortunately, he was happy to explain everything in detail.

It was quite an education. I didn't want to forget any of it, so I took plenty of notes. He told me things I had never heard about before. Smart, creative methods that have a big effect on income. Even when companies know about some of these methods, there are reasons why they don't tell them to their home workers. You have to discover them for yourself or learn them from someone who knows.

I started applying these new methods along with what I already knew about envelope stuffing. It made an enormous difference. Within weeks I was making more money than ever before. And it actually took less work. I had more time than ever to enjoy the money I was making.

All it takes is a few hours a day to make more money than many people earn with full-time jobs. My special combination of effective methods and shortcuts makes it easy. I call it the Easy Home Paycheck System. It takes advantage of existing companies that already are paying people all over the country. Anyone can receive this pay once they know what to do.

The company owners would be delighted to have more people using my methods. They can't figure out how I earn such big checks, but they love paying them to me because their business benefits in proportion. Everything is honest and above board. It's a home business that you can be proud of.

All the secrets of my Easy Home Paycheck System are explained in my book. Just follow my clear, step-by-step instructions and start getting those checks yourself. Once the system is set up, it's like cranking a money machine. Work a few hours and take the rest of the day off. That's what I do. It's a wonderful life, and I especially enjoy being able to help others achieve it.
Two Free Gifts To Get You Going

It's important to start with a good high-paying program that has no income limit. I do more than just recommend one. As a free gift to my readers, I include a special prepaid application form for one of the best paying mailing programs. Through special arrangements, you can join this exceptional program absolutely free. You will never have to pay the $39.00 registration fee. Just cut the registration form from my book, complete it, and mail it to the company. They'll send your starting materials right to you. Before you know it, you can be receiving paychecks every week.

My second free gift will get you into a top dollar-per-envelope program. With so many phony offers around, you can have a hard time finding a legitimate program of this type. I'll save you the trouble. I know one company that truly does pay one dollar for each envelope like they say. Their reliable program requires a $35.00 fee to join. But not for you.

My book includes a special prepaid application form for this desirable program. Cut it out, complete it, and mail it in. You pay nothing! They'll send your starting materials absolutely free. Just follow the directions and get paid one hundred dollars by return mail for each hundred envelopes you submit to them. Plus they pay an extra allowance for the shipping cost.
A Guarantee You Can Trust

My book costs just $29.95 plus shipping. That's a small investment compared to the moneyyou can soon be making. But I don't want you to feel you are taking any chances with your hard earned money. That's why I back my book with a foolproof, see-for-yourself guarantee.

When you get my book, look it over and make sure you can make money as easily as I say. If you have any doubt at all, simply return the book within sixty days.

(continues)

Figure 17-2. (*continued*)

I'll immediately refund your full $29.95. There is no requirement that you try any program or do anything else. This is a true, no-nonsense money-back guarantee. And there's more.

Your two prepaid application forms will be accepted without question if submitted within sixty days. You can join either one or both programs without paying any fee. I guarantee it or your money back.

My guarantee is backed by a real person who you can talk to if necessary. If anything is missing or you have a question about the guarantee, you can call the customer service phone number in the front of my book and talk to a real person, not an answering machine. That's the best way I know to make sure any problems are promptly handled. It's one more assurance that you can depend on what I say.
Start Getting Your Share

I'm thankful for how much "envelope stuffing" has solved my money problems and brightened my life. I'm glad to be able to help you get in on this easy and honest way to make money. Everything you need to know is in "Secrets of Stuffing Envelopes". The methods that bring me hundreds of dollars a week can work just as well for you. See for yourself.

Simply complete the order form and mail it with your payment to the order fullfillment company I have selected below for faster service. You can't go wrong with my unbeatable money-back guarantee. Put my Easy Home Paycheck System to work and start enjoying the good life. You deserve it.

Sincerely,

Linda Applebee

PS- When the two high paying programs have enough people, I must stop including forms that let my readers join free. I'll return your order if I receive it too late. Hurry, I don't want you to miss out.

Thank You For The Kind Letters

"Your book is just what I was looking for. I heard about stuffing envelopes, but I didn't know how to get started. Now I know what to do."
-Wendy Koehn, Illinois

"Thank you for your wonderful book. I was skeptical at first, but it really works. I received two checks already. Next week I plan to do twice as much."
-David Horton, Arizona

"I thought envelope stuffing was totally fake until I read your book. It turned out to be just like you said. I'm going to get started right away"
-Greg Morrison, South Carolina

"I was glad to finally learn the truth about envelope stuffing. I wasted a lot of money before, but now I can make up for it."
-Sheila Heffington, Texas

"Thank you for your terrific book. It's just what I needed. Finally, I know exactly what to do."
-Cindy Trubak, Tennessee

"I had to write and tell you that I just received my first check today. I can't tell you how happy I am. Everything you said is true."
-Carolyn Padgett, Oregon

Purchase Now Online!

or
use this form to order by mail

—————————cut here——————————————————————

eCreations   #305
P.O. Box 22073
San Diego, CA 92192-2073

(continues)

Figure 17-2. (*continued*)

( ) Yes, I want to learn how to get paid like you as an independent contractor. Enclosed is $29.95 plus $3.00 for postage and handling ($32.95 total) for "Secrets of Stuffing Envelopes" with the Easy Home Paycheck System and free application forms.* I am protected by your genuine no-nonsense money-back guarantee.

*Checks may be made payable to ECreations

Name_____

Address_____

City, State, Zip_____

——————-cut here————————————————————————

_____

No Removal Instructions Are Necessary- This Is A One Time Mailing.
You Will Not Hear From Us Again.

_____

Figure 17-3 shows obfuscation in action! This e-mail touts a work-at-home plan, but few will be able to penetrate the rhetoric. On second thought, make that *nobody* will be able to penetrate the rhetoric.

Figure 17-3. Obfuscation in action!

Subj:	**HomeWorkers Urgently Needed p**
Date:	12:49:18 AM Pacific Daylight Time
From:	N22553@review-casino.com
To:	snigs@aol.com

Home Employment
Work the hours You want
Work from the comfort of your own home or Office
Many Companies to work with

Assemble Products
click on this link
and type you email address in the message body and hit send and
your email addresses will be removed within 24 hours
&&&&&&&&&&&&&&&&&&&&&&&&&&&&&&&&&&&&&&&& Note
that The speaker-hearer's linguistic intuition Is unspecified with respect to No dis-
tinctness in the sense of distinctive feature theory. Were only relatively inaccessible
to movement, The theory of syntactic features developed earlier Is to be regarded
as the extended C-command discussed in connection with (34). This suggests
that The descriptive power of the base component Does not readily tolerate the
strong generative capacity of the theory. It must be emphasized, once again, that
A subset of English sentences interesting on quite independent grounds Suffices to
account for A general convention regarding the forms of the grammar. Let us continue to suppose that Any associated supporting element Does not affect the
structure of a descriptive fact. On our assumptions, The notion of level of gram-
maticalness Appears to correlate rather closely with the system of base rules exclusive of the lexicon. Thus The fundamental error of regarding functional notions as
categorical Is not to be considered in determining the levels of acceptability from
fairly high (eg (99a)) to virtual gibberish (eg (98d)). By combining adjunctions
and certain deformations, This selection ally introduced contextual feature May
remedy and, at the same time, eliminate the traditional practice of grammarians.
&&&&&&&&&&&&&&&&&&&&&&&&&&&&&&&&&&&&&&&

For the e-mail in Figure 17-4, production is paramount over clarity.

Figure 17-4. When production is paramount to clarity.

Subj:	**Incoming: your link to business technology**
Date:	8/22 2:50:03 AM Eastern Daylight Time
From:	HewlettPackard@hplj.m0.net (Hewlett-Packard)
Reply-to:	HewlettPackard@hplj.m0.net
To:	HGLEWIS1@aol.com

Click here for current HP promotions.

The false cry of urgency in Figure 17-5 immediately destroys credibility.

Figure 17-5. A false cry of urgency.

Subj:	**Urgent: The Fair Credit Reporting Act mxzbrld szglpv51890767 mxzbrld**
Date:	8/22 4:59:40 AM Eastern Daylight Time
From:	ConsumerInfoListsszglpv51890767@mxzbrld.com
To:	hglewis1@aol.com

How would you like to have PERFECT CREDIT?
Thanks to the U.S. Govt. and The Fair Credit Reporting Act
YOU CAN Quickly Restore Your Credit Rating!

Find Out what the Credit Bureaus DON'T want You to Know!

Click Here for FREE Information.

What is missing in Figure 17-6? Credibility? Clarity? Or both?

Figure 17-6. What is missing here?

Subj:	200% return in less than 90 days! 15600
Date:	8/22 3:16:36 AM Eastern Daylight Time
From:	larrywil456@wanadoo.fr
Reply-to:	lance454@wanadoo.fr
To:	lance454@wanadoo.fr

===
Attention: An "english" speaking representative will be contacting
you to verify your correct mailing information prior to shipping
you your FREE special report(s). A valid phone number is required!
We apologize, but this investment opportunity does not apply
to "United States, India and Pakistan residents at this time.
===

Currency Trading Made Simple!

Do You Have The Yen To Be a A Millionaire?

200% return in less than 90 days!

Unique Strategy Trading in the International Currency Markets!

Largest MarketPlace in the World!

Get our Reports, Charts and Strategies on the U.S. Dollar vs
Japanese yen and euro.
Example:

A $5,000 Investment in the Euro vs the Dollar, "properly positioned",
on 09/29/00 could have returned $12,500.00 on 10/19/00.

For your FREE information package, contact us today.

click here to visit our website...now!!

The e-mail in Figure 17-7 has, as vernacular puts it, "everything
but the kitchen sink." While some people will find it too formidable
to penetrate, others will regard it as a travel bible.

Figure 17-7. Everything but the kitchen sink.

Subj:	**The Insider from Travelocity.com**
Date:	12:46:17 PM Central Daylight Time
From:	feedback@travelocity.m0.net (Travelocity.com)
Reply-to:	feedback@travelocity.m0.net
To:	DRAGONELLE@aol.com

Air, Car, and Hotel Reservations
- General Reservation Questions
- Air Reservation Questions
- Schedule Change Information

- Hotel Reservation Questions
- Car/Rail Reservation Questions
- Credit Card Security Questions
- Travel Agency Directory Questions

(continues)

Figure 17-7. (*continued*)

Ticketing and Delivery

Registration, Log-In and Security

Accessing Travelocity.com

Other Travelocity.com Features
- Fare Watcher Questions
- Flight Paging
- Travelocity.com Newsletter
- Shop with an agent

Travelocity Preferred Program
Last Minute Deals
- General
- Types of Products
- Before You Purchase - Availability

- Before You Purchase - Pricing
- Before You Purchase - Special Requests
- While You Purchase - Buying the Package
- While You Purchase - Policies/ Procedures
- While You Purchase - Security
- After You Purchase

Helpful Information - Travel Resources

Non U.S., Canada, Germany & UK users

AOL and Mac OS Users

Information for SABRE Travel Agents

If all this exposition, all these explanations, all these strange and arcane terms, all these wild predictions and chest-thumpings, all these projections that turn out to be either ridiculously understated or arrogantly overstated ... if all you've read and absorbed in these pages leads only to bewilderment because the future of e-mail is changing even as we enter that future...take comfort in the next three words:

You aren't alone.

We're in this together, we communicators and communicator-poseurs. We're seeing the rules coalesce before our eyes.

And, pioneers that we are, we congratulate ourselves for being present at the birth and spurting growth of the most magnificent medium of force-communication ever given to those of us who hope we'll learn how to use it effectively.

To all of us: Aren't we lucky to be here, so soon after the launch? And aren't we even luckier, watching and profiting from the new rules that can cause our cash registers and phones to ring a little more often?!

"And in conclusion, ladies and gentlemen . . ."

The horrible events of September 11, 2001, and the ensuing transmission of anthrax bacteria through the mail, had a profound effect on every facet of force-communication.

Suddenly, as though a giant switch were turned, the terrorist attack decimated the effectiveness of conventional direct mail and focused both consumer and marketer attention on e-mail. Advertisers who had chuckled at the concept of using e-mail as a primary medium made frantic preparations for either augmenting their mailed promotions with e-mail . . . or switching entirely.

Predictable Results

Three results were predictable: The first was e-mail glut. List companies reveled in new clientele who wanted bulk rather than selectivity.

Research companies revised upward their predictions of both dollar volume and number of e-mail transmissions, by billions.

The second result was the flip-side of e-mail glut. Recipients became more selective, more aggressive in opting out, and less attentive to individual messages.

The nasty realization that everybody is an expert became apparent when many who had read whopping success stories in the trade publications assumed every road was paved with gold. But the rules of force-communication are both absolute and ferocious. We're mired deep in the Age of Skepticism, and savvy marketers cater to reality, not to what *they* want.

And that realization led to the third result—marketers demanding a CPA approach instead of CPM. To some, who had been told e-mail results paralleled picking up gold nuggets off a dry creek bed, that third realization has become a belated revelation.

A study by IMT Strategies, an online market research organization, indicated a 77 percent rate of commercial e-mail deletion without reading the message, while 48 percent of respondents said they did read e-mails from senders to whom they had given permission. As e-mails become hypercompetitive, future success or failure obviously rests on the shoulders of marketers who can convince recipients, "You asked for this."

The "Who Sent This and Why?" Question, Squared

In e-mail's early days, the "Spam!" accusation was limited to a relatively few noisy recipients who either sought public attention or clamored for legislative controls, or both. Today's reaction is more subtle and more deadly. An individual signs up for a newsletter or a free offer (often "free" except for a $7.95 shipping/handling charge). The whole purpose of reader recruitment is, in a great number of instances, to be able to claim: "You opted in for whatever message we, or however many marketers rent your name from us, want to send you."

So the day's e-mail becomes not a controlled Arabian bazaar in which a visitor decides to wander from tent to tent, looking for bargains, but a wilderness in which the plaintive question "Who sent this and why?" bleeds over to other e-mails.

The one-to-one medium creates a one-against-all mentality. Opt-out rates rise. E-mail, even worthy e-mail, goes unread.

Forrester Research says more than half of new users think they're getting too many e-mail messages. (Don't let that one throw you, because *far more* than half of television viewers think they're putting up with too many commercials; yet that older medium survives even as cynical stations and networks constantly increase the number of commercial minutes in each hour's programming.)

E-mail's origins occasionally pop up to haunt it. The earliest e-mail marketers simply imported regular direct mail into this new marketing phenomenon, just as the earliest television advertising was radio copy with pictures added. The practice of putting an e-mail label on direct mail still exists. That may be one reason many, many critics claim e-mail is inefficient as a parallel to "cold list" mailings whose purpose is to recruit *new* buyers or donors or affiliates.

The claim has merit if applied to inefficient use of e-mail. Too, unsorted names generally aren't as valuable or malleable as those who have asked for e-mail. They can't be. But the cost factor is a potent siren song, and even if response percentages are minimal the results can be profitable.

Now, what's wrong with that last sentence? What's wrong isn't the truth of it but, rather, the danger implicit in reducing this exquisite one-to-one medium to bulk solicitation. That creates a sibling danger—the danger of destroying potential receptivity, which boils over to damage all e-mailers.

Pretend You're the Recipient

Many a message comes from marketers who not only aren't representative of the target-individuals to whom they're e-mailing; they also arrogantly refuse to join that segment of the marketplace, even to sample its environment.

Everyone knows e-mail is cheap, efficient, and fast. That, to too many marketers, is the alpha and omega of media decision-making. And why do I say "too many" marketers? Because each marketer who damages a medium causes harm to other marketers who do understand that medium. I suppose we should be puzzled that so many professionals in the world of advertising and sales promotion not only don't understand how logical it is, but also haven't grasped how easy it is, for e-mail to be exquisitely tailored to be *interactive*. E-mails generated by those marketers are doubly damaged, because that magical word "interactive" is the seed-word for an even more miraculous word—*rapport*.

So out go messages to more than 30 million America Online subscribers. The messages are sent as a 100 percent download. And what comes up on the screen? A dire warning from America Online. A bold headline says either "Warning: If you don't know who sent you this e-mail, be cautious in downloading this file" . . . or "Do you know who sent you this e-mail?" The warning goes on to suggest the download could damage the computer or might be an objectionable picture.

Click! Millions of fingers on millions of mice avoid millions of messages that, had they been constructed as conventional messages with an *attached* download, would have survived. The sender doesn't have a clue because his or her online address is so-and-so-@-company.com, and AOL's structures aren't part of market research or planning.

Other demonstrations of nonprofessionalism abound. An ancient rule of salesmanship dictates: When the prospect says "yes," quit selling. Out goes an e-mail. The offer is clear enough, but the means for saying yes is buried so deeply in the text the individual clicks away.

Here comes another e-mail. Nothing about the offer requires an illustration, but somebody has told the marketer: "You need pictures to make your e-mail contemporary." The screen sits, waiting for something to happen. And what happens is a click to the next message.

But every mistake e-mailers make (other than those relating to specific technology) has been made hundreds of thousands of times before, in newspapers, magazines, broadcast, and direct mail. Ineffective use of any medium in no way should suggest that the medium itself is ineffective.

So this book ends with a three-part plea that pertains to all force-communication and has become especially significant to e-mail:

1. Don't let production technology substitute for salesmanship.

2. Always ask, "If I were reading this instead of sending it, would it convince me to respond?" . . . and answer that question honestly.

3. Once you have a solid contact with anyone, whether business or consumer, treasure and nurture the relationship.

No one can guarantee that with those elements in place, you'll positively succeed. But it certainly is likely that without those elements in place, you'll positively fail.

Good luck to us all as we develop, cultivate, and (we hope) profit from the most dynamic medium we ever have been lucky enough to exploit.

A Potpourri of Tips

• For business-to-business e-mails, if you are torn between text and rich media, untear yourself and opt for text. Response rates may be higher for rich media, but many companies fear viruses and prohibit allowing rich media, streaming media, or e-mails with attachments to get through to employees. If you positively feel that rich media is the answer, test a link in your e-mail, sending prospects to a Web site that has rich media advertising or mini-movie marketing.

• An expiration date always helps to encourage response. And the more specific the expiration date, the better the response. So "Reply by midnight Friday, May 25" has greater power than "Reply by Friday, May 25," which in turn has greater power than "Reply by May 25."

- When recruiting customers, clients, or donors, keep the message short. Message length can increase in ratio to the number of times the prospect has contacted *you*.

- In e-mails to businesses, rich media or a "produced" message may be less effective than straight text. Why? Because straight text is less likely to give an immediate impression that you are trying to sell something.

- If you have a sweepstakes or prize offer, plug it on your home page. Don't assume that e-mail announcements alone will seize the attention of every name on the list. Get the interaction any way you can, because interaction is the key to fragile customer attention for your next e-mail.

- The bulk of consumer response usually arrives within forty-eight hours. That is faster than business response, because business recipients aren't as likely to dedicate time for immediate response, especially on Mondays and Fridays.

- The key question in deciding whether or not to put your company name in the subject line is: Where did the name to which you're e-mailing come from?

- Sending an entire text message in an unusual color will seize attention. The trade-off is that the message is quickly recognizable as advertising. Whether this will be a positive or negative effect depends on your relationship with the recipient.

- Mirror print advertising from a production point of view when e-mailing to seniors. That means, above all, using easily readable fonts. (This isn't a bad idea for e-mailing to everybody, provided that it still looks like e-mail.) But *don't* make the mistake of letting your image be one of catering exclusively to older people, because they will resent the suggestion as much as younger prospects might, albeit on a different level.

- Excessive tailoring and excessive targeting can supress response, not only from the fringes but also from the group at whom the message is targeted, because they may feel the communication is an invasion of privacy.

- Be careful of overdependence on a single database factor. You can bypass eclectic tastes by catering to only one taste.

- Seldom is sending the identical message to customers and prospects an ideal communications technique. One exception that makes the conclusion valid as "seldom" instead of "never": treating prospects as though they actually are customers. (Amateurish attempts to do this invariably result in a spam accusation.)

- E-mail that looks as though a business associate sent it may be the most effective marketing use of this medium. That means eschewing both heavy production and verbosity. But never forget that for maximum efficiency, send e-mail only when you can claim both relationship and relevance.

- If you send news releases to media, be sure the media regard them as _news_. Don't claim your speculations are facts: Editors are wise to "vaporware" announcements. Candor goes a long way. Avoid those adjectival superlatives that turn your release into a transparent piece of advertising. The acceptance rate will go up if your news actually is news.

- Any e-mail to a handheld device has to be terse and pointed. Otherwise, not only will there be opt-outs, but the negative word of mouth will be fierce. As short as attention spans are on the Web, they're leisurely compared with the same person's attention span on a Palm Pilot.

• Don't offer big prizes for opt-ins. For every legitimate opt-in, you may recruit a dozen freebie-hunters who have no interest other than in acquiring something for nothing. Viral mail becomes a curse rather than a blessing when an opt-in offer is overly generous.

• Content is more important than production in *any* newsletter, whether printed or e-mailed. The first item should be a startler.

• Don't limit a sweepstakes to new names. Doing that can outrage the best names on any list—your active customers.

• When an e-mail makes an offer that strains credulity, having it signed by what appears to be a representative of the sender adds verisimilitude and credibility.

• The bigger a sweepstakes grand prize, the greater the extended time before the drawing can be. To keep the pot boiling, allow additional entries for additional actions or purchases.

• Don't drive direct-mail leads to your home page if you want to capture the e-mail address. Send them to a URL that displays an immediate, clear, irresistible offer. After all, by establishing a detour to the home page, you're actually in a *three*-step conversion.

• For verisimilitude, when e-mailing on a reciprocal basis with another marketer, don't link to the other company's home page. Link to a page that has the special offer mentioned in the e-mail.

• When renting e-mail lists, a key anti-spam-accusation question is: "Have parallel companies e-mailed this list before, and what kind of response did they get?" Two assumptions are vital for giving value to both the question and the answer to it: (1)

Is the answer to your question truthful? and (2) If the answer is truthful, has the list been e-mailed so heavily the cream is out of the bottle?

• Acknowledge every e-mail referral with a thank-you e-mail, immediately. Equally immediate should be your contact to the referred individual. If you aren't ready to do that, delay the program until you are.

• Two of the most foolproof techniques for avoiding the spam accusation are: (1) relevance to the individual's own business or lifestyle, and (2) avoiding the appearance of having produced just another sales pitch.

• The shorter the message, the less likely it is that anyone will regard it as spam.

• Make it both easy and profitable for recipients to respond. That means including the capability for your target individuals to separate automated responses from inquiries and comments. This not only helps reduce opt-outs but also maintains the image of customer control, a valuable component of "virtual rapport."

• If you think _any_ e-mail has a problem establishing or maintaining rapport, you understand that the volume, intensity, and potential irritation potential of the medium warrant a thoughtful "How do I couch this?" preanalysis.

• An underused tool is an occasional thank-you or a note from the top executive saying, "Just want to tell you how much we appreciate your being a member of our family," with no commercial overtone.

• Text tends to outpull HTML when your message suggests _urgency_. HTML tends to outpull text when your message suggests _artistry_.

• The more technically oriented your targets are the more likely it is they will prefer text to HTML. That seems wrong on its face, but many who have tested both types or sent both simultaneously seem to believe HTML works best with people who aren't technically adept. Test it.

• E-mail isn't a Web site. Loading an e-mail message with photographs and graphic elements can be counterproductive if the e-mail seems to be a mini-Web site. Many e-marketers report better results from e-mail that builds a desire to "click here," thereby taking the individual to the site.

• If you want your HTML or rich media e-mail message to reach everybody, don't assume universal HTML compatibility or knowledge. Prepare the message in a text version as well.

• When you have sent several e-mail offers a recipient has opened but not acted on, test one of the following:

1. A more dynamic, more aggressive approach

2. A discount, tied strongly to an expiration date

3. A more personalized, more one-to-one message, using guilt or exclusivity as the motivator

4. A change of format, either to or from HTML or rich media

• Quickly and constantly remind your target of your relationship.

• Keep replies to e-mail from customers or prospects brief but friendly. And always reconfirm the customer's e-mail address.

- The classic marketing truth that emotion outpulls intellect is as valuable a sales weapon as any e-mailer can aim.

- An expiration date always helps elicit a response.

- Don't extend specificity to inclusion of the recipient's postal code in an e-mail solicitation. Many who harbor no negative thoughts about seeing their town in the subject line react negatively to a postal code, which implies: "These people have investigated me."

- Advertising is adjectival. Advertising writers look for adjectives and often subordinate other parts of speech. Unless you want your message to reflect an advertising intent, play down the adjectives.

- When renting names, insist on the same merge-purge privileges that extend to names rented for direct mail. One individual may not only have three or four online addresses but also be carried on numerous lists.

- If you require a password, ask yourself why. Customers know they don't need a password to order from a printed catalog or to shop in a store. Why do they need a password from you? Give them a reason that seems to benefit them, not you.

- Why ask for city, state, and ZIP code, when ZIP code alone tells you the city and state?

- Don't be so in love with your home page that you constantly link e-mail to that page, regardless of what the specific offer might be. Send visitors where they want to go, not where you're happiest.

• Don't wait until the customer is in the shopping cart to disclose the price. That's not only a sign of cowardice; it's stupid sales psychology.

• When emphasizing discount, it's "20%," not "20 percent." When the message is upscale or genteel, it's "twenty percent."

• One absolute assumption any marketer should value is: Bury your own ego; revere and cater to your target's ego.

• "I" is superior to "We" for establishing a relationship. "We" is superior to "I" for assuming corporate responsibility. Including both within the same message is completely logical, as long as the test clarifies who "I" am and who "We" are.

• When enthusiasm goes over the top and becomes either shrill or implausible, it then is suspect. Reader enthusiasm diminishes.

• Synergy seems to apply when a marketer e-mails a customer with news of a forthcoming direct-mail package or printed catalog, and/or highlights from that direct-mail package or catalog. Those who employ this technique say response to both goes up. Certainly, the inexpensive procedure is worth testing.

• The more specific the expiration date, the greater the verisimilitude. So "Good until midnight Saturday, September 7" has greater impact than "Good through Saturday, September 7."

• In an e-mail newsletter, when including a preview of a forthcoming revelation, position that preview early in the text. Unusual type treatment may help grab the eye. Leaving this vital component to the end can result in many recipients, bored by apparent sameness, not seeing it at all and concluding that receiving the newsletter isn't worth the continuing effort.

- A daily Newsletter will generate opt-outs at a far greater rate than a daily Brief News Flash.

- Don't let enthusiasm for the medium lead you to overestimating the reader anticipation a preliminary announcement can generate. Test against including actual offers in every e-mail.

- The natural indicator that you're e-mailing too frequently is a surge of opt-outs. But don't necessarily relate the opt-outs to how often you e-mail. More often, the cause is content, not frequency.

- Being able to determine a winning message isn't the only benefit of e-mail's quick response. The marriage of database and technology offers another: Send e-mail when specific targets are most likely to respond. Accucast suggests lunchtime as profitable for sending consumer e-mails, because many people catch up on reading their e-mail while eating snacks at their desks.

- Understand the difference between a generalization and a rule. Generally, Monday and Friday e-mails to business recipients are subject to quick deletion without reading. But that is _generally_ and _subject to._ Testing, and only testing, will prove whether or not your specific type of message works as well on Monday and Friday . . . or even better.

- When deciding whether to use rich media or plain text, first test the two against each other. If that is impossible, target and hit to the best of your professional ability. Then refine and massage the message.

- Rich media require no more technical capability on the part of the message recipient than the ability to receive text. Don't avoid rich media because you fear the possibility of recipient ignorance of the technology; rather, testing rich media against text should generate a conclusion based on the cost-versus-response ratio. So test only a segment of the list when sending a message in rich media. This conclusion isn't based only on technology. Testing also has to relate to effectiveness, since so many prior tests to business targets have given the edge to text, both in cost and in response.

- Rich media's difference is that they are an *experience*; text is a *message*. Is what you have to say of quick significance or importance? This suggests text. Does it require graphics or sound, as movies or CDs do? This suggests rich media.

- A "click-through rate" in no way parallels a response rate, any more than opening a direct-mail envelope is parallel to sending an order.

- Most experts seem to agree that technology-driven viral marketing is considerably less effective than relationship-driven viral marketing. Including a place or procedure for a personal note validates the forwarded message.

- The ultimate tip is: Test. And when you encounter your next marketing project, test again.

Index

About the Author

This is the twenty-sixth book by the renowned "Creative Guru" who has written e-mail and advertising copy for, and consulted with, clients and advertising agencies across the planet. According to Herschell Gordon Lewis, this is far and away his most important book "because it includes new rules for using the most dynamic medium ever made available to marketers."

Mr. Lewis is former chairman of Communicomp, a full-service direct marketing agency. He now heads Lewis Enterprises, through which he writes and consults individually. His background includes more than twenty years as adjunct lecturer to graduate classes in Mass Communications, Roosevelt University, Chicago.

Mr. Lewis is the author of the classic *On the Art of Writing Copy*. His other books include *Marketing Mayhem; Copywriting Secrets and Tactics; Direct Marketing Strategies and Tactics; Big Profits from*

Small Budget Advertising; Direct Mail Copy That Sells; More Than You Ever Wanted to Know About Mail Order Advertising; How to Make Your Advertising Twice as Effective at Half the Cost; Open Me Now!; Sales Letters That Sizzle; Silver Linings—Selling to the Expanding Mature Market; The Businessman's Guide to Advertising and Sales Promotion; How to Write Powerful Fund Raising Letters; The Advertising Age Handbook of Advertising—well, you get the idea.

For 200 consecutive issues, Mr. Lewis wrote the monthly feature "Creative Strategies" for *Direct Marketing* magazine. He currently writes "Better Letters" for *Selling* newsletter, "Curmudgeon-at-Large" for *Direct*, and is the copy columnist for *Catalog Age*. He also writes "Copy Class" for the UK publication *Direct Marketing International*, catalog critiques for the UK publication *Catalogue & eBusiness*, and occasional creative features for *Internet Retailer*.

For years, Mr. Lewis conducted the copy workshop at the International Direct Marketing Symposium, Montreux, Switzerland, and he has appeared frequently at the Pan-Pacific Symposium in Sydney, Australia.

He also has presented seminars and workshops in countries such as England, France, Spain, New Zealand, Norway, Denmark, Sweden, Switzerland, Brazil, Singapore, South Africa, Austria, Mexico, Holland, Belgium, Germany, Hong Kong, Indonesia, and Dubai. He has been named to the Florida Direct Marketing Association Hall of Fame.

Mr. Lewis is a resident of Fort Lauderdale, Florida. He is a tennis player and scuba diver.